YOU CAN'T UN-RING *The* BELL

Linda Fay Clark

You Can't Un-ring the Bell

Book II of Coming Home to Wiswell series

By Linda Fay Clark
(C) Copyright by Linda Fay Clark
ISBN 978-1-09832-247-2 eBook 978-1-09832-248-9

June 2020

All of the characters in my book are real people, though I have assigned fictitious names to just a few. All the stories in my book are absolutely (mostly) true. A little enhancement is good for the soul…and for storytelling. While the focus of this book is primarily on the latter part of the Great Depression and on through World War II, there are some family events included that were outside that time period; in fact, some take place well before I was born, but were passed on to me by my parents.

The reader should keep in mind that the information herein was gleaned and reported "as seen through the eyes of a child", but some has been further expounded upon in retrospect by an 80-plus year-old, and may be less accurate than the child's version. However, this book was written for enjoyment more than for historical accuracy.

Dedication

To Mama, who, if not the inventor, then the frequent purveyor of peach tree tea, of which I was oft the recipient. Perhaps that is why I grew up to earn several academic degrees and was promoted to Associate Professor and awarded tenure at Murray State University—**twice!** I retired from the United States Army as a Lieutenant Colonel, with 20 years of service. As a Certified Nurse-Midwife, I have delivered more than 3,000 babies. The Governor of Kentucky recognized me for making valuable contributions to the Commonwealth by awarding the prestigious title Kentucky Colonel to me (which has nothing to do with fried chicken.) I previously published several articles in professional journals and my first book, *Coming Home to Wiswell.* In addition, my husband Ray and I raised four beautiful and successful sons.

Contents

Wiswell   1

The Cliques   13

My First Hamburger   17

Papa's First (and Last) Home-Made Biscuits   21

Poplin, of the "Turnip Green Patch Story"   26

The Step Mothers   36

Mama's Mouse Traps   42

Jewel's New Hat   48

Change of Dinner Venue   52

The Runt Pig   55

Christmas in Wiswell   61

Fourth Monday in March Mule Day   69

Games We Played   73

Swapping Knives   77

My First Boyfriend   79

My Pet Rabbit…that wasn't   83

Contents

Stripping tobacco for Christmas Money   88

Hog Killing   92

Wilkerson Farm Life   97

Wiswell Country Store   108

The Wiswell News Column   115

The Big Old Bull   120

Vacation Bible School   123

The Dough Boy   126

The Wiswell Fly Boys of World War II   133

From Normandy to the Battle of the Bulge*   137

A Troop Train Romance   142

Sunday afternoon Sports   148

A Gift for a Gift   153

Twilight   155

Wiswell

In 1897, a little 8- year-old girl named Virginia, wrote a letter to the editor of the New York Sun newspaper, and asked him if there really was a Santa Claus. She wrote that some of her little friends had told her that there wasn't a Santa Claus, that it was just her parents who put the presents under the tree. She said she asked her daddy if this was true. His answer was simply "If you see it in the Sun, it's true." So that was why she was directing her question to the Sun.

The editor published his answer in his newspaper saying, "Yes, Virginia. There really is a Santa Claus. He exists as certainly as love, generosity, and devotion exists…which gives life its highest beauty and joy."

To borrow his phrase, I would say, "Yes, there really is a Wiswell, and in that community the people (just like Santa Claus) exemplify the spirit of love, generosity, and devotion, to neighbors, friends, and family; and if occasion arises, also to strangers, or anyone in need. This, too, gives life its highest beauty and joy. Though the people there, in Wiswell, themselves, suffered during the Great Depression and on through WWII (which is the main time-focus of this book), they gave life its beauty and joy through neighborliness, and they would share whatever they had, whether it was food, money, work, prayers, or their time. If a farmer was sick or suffered a great tragedy at about the time of harvest, or perhaps at planting time, or any time in-between, the local farmers would get together and complete all his farm work, and without being asked. And mow his lawn, for good measure. In situations like that there would be horses or mules, with whatever equipment was necessary for the task.

One innovative farmer had a new-fangled tractor. It was bright orange with black letters reading Allis-Chalmers. It made so much noise—chug, chug, almost like a train---that its owner, Mr. Elmo Fain, had to operate it in a separate field, as it frightened the horses, if too close. And it had drawbacks. No one knew for sure, but it was rumored that it cost $1,000!

"He'll have to sell a lot of tobacco to pay for that," someone predicted.

"It'll never replace a good sturdy mule," said another.

An additional problem with the tractor was the fact that it ran on gas; that cost money, too. "Can't just feed hay and oats to that contraption," someone else pointed out. "The price of gas keeps going up, and it will continue to climb as there are more and more motor vehicles using it. The last time I was in Murray it was already 21 cents per gallon.

"But if anyone can make a go of it, Elmo can," he conceded.

"They say that little boy of his, Billy Pat, can already drive that thing. Can you believe that? He's not knee high to a grasshopper."

"Oh yes, in fact when Elmo bought that tractor, Billy Pat drove it home, with Elmo driving his truck right behind him. Why that kid can't be more than eight or nine years old."

Reed Brandon voiced his opinion, "I say that's a good thing, getting the boy interested in farming, because he's always acting like he's flying an airplane. He's going to break his neck if he keeps jumping out of haylofts or tobacco barns, waving his arms like they were wings. Maybe the tractor will make him forget about flying."

Little did they know that while the boy was driving the tractor, he was pretending it was an airplane. It would have surprised them even more if they had known that he would grow up to be a pilot and teach flying at the prestigious Embry-Riddle Aeronautical University.

The tractor was productive, since so much work could be done quicker, but it was questionable as to its practicality. Many of the farmers speculated that it would never amount to much.

In 1943 there was another little 8-year-old inquisitive girl, named Linda Fay, who also had questions, though she didn't seek the answers by writing to an editor. (Perhaps those of you who read *Coming Home to Wiswell* may remember her contributions to our local newspaper, however, by writing a fictitious birth announcement that was actually published. Perhaps that was the very first example of Fake News.) This child faced life with an appetite for learning about the world in which she lived, and often learned things "the hard way." That little girl grew up, then grew old, and finally, now has had the courage to write about her memories.

When I was that little girl, my grandparents and Aunt Margie lived about a mile from us, and Papa and my brothers often helped them on their farm. By the same token, Granny and Granddaddy could often be found helping on our farm.

Farm life was hard, and the wife and daughters worked in the field alongside the men folk. But a while before noon the women would slip away to the house to prepare dinner, which is what they called the noon meal. The energy that was generated by a good hearty breakfast would begin to diminish by this time and needed to be replenished by a substantial dinner.

In fact, enough food would be cooked at noon to have plenty of leftovers for supper, negating the need to fire up the cook stove full blast, for the evening meal.

In the late morning, the heat was sweltering, but a blazing fire was started in the wood-burning cook stove, and a bountiful meal was made ready. The smell of frying chicken and country sausage filled the air. Hot biscuits, browned just so, and a big pone of corn bread cooked in a cast iron skillet, were taken from the oven. After removing the bread, Mama might take several sweet potatoes, jab holes in them with a fork to allow steam to vent and rub them in bacon grease and place them in the oven. As the fire died away the sweet potatoes would gradually cook, and be ready to eat at supper, with butter, brown sugar, and maybe a sprinkle of cinnamon.

Fresh, red tomatoes were peeled —always peeled, then sliced, enough to fill a platter. (Our city relatives sliced tomatoes, leaving the peel on, which we viewed as taking a lazy shortcut.) New cabbage from the garden, cooked with bacon, and an overflowing dish of crispy fried okra were placed on one end of the table. A huge dish of hot buttered corn-on-the cob was placed in the center of the table, alongside a bowl of fried new potatoes with onions. A bucket of cool milk was retrieved from the cistern, where it had stayed fresh, and big glassfuls were poured and placed beside each plate. But the big bowl of butter beans seemed to be the focal point of the whole spread.

Mama took great pride in her butter beans, for she considered them a family heirloom. Each fall, some were allowed to dry on the bush, and seeds were saved from the current crop to be planted next spring. She said the lineage of the seed could be traced back to her great-great-grand-mother Adams, and they had been passed on down with each generation. My sisters and I were charged with keeping the tradition.

"Someday you'll be planting butter beans that came from these same seed," she said in a solemn tone of voice, as she held out a handful, which were of perfect shape and color. "And when you have a little girl of your own, you will need to save some seed for her, and tell her this story of her ancestors who always planted these very same seed." I felt very honored to be trusted with such a monumental duty—to be the guardian of the treasured seeds, taking care to preserve them for posterity.

"You must not let them die out," she stressed the importance of our responsibility.

By the time dinner was ready, the sun would be straight overhead, so the men in the field knew it was noon, but they wanted to take advantage of every minute to continue working, so they waited until the sound of the dinner bell signaled that it was time to come to the house. The food would already be on the table, ready to eat. No working time lost.

The dinner bell hung on a post in the back yard. To me it looked like a smaller version of the Liberty Bell in a picture that I had seen in my brother's history book. It hung high so the sound could carry to the farthest field, wherever the men might be working. Pulling the rope that hung down caused the clapper to clang against the inside of the metal bell, which produced vibrations, that made the ringing sound. My brother who was three years older and a little taller than me always got to ring the dinner bell to signal to the men that it was time to come to eat. When I wanted to pull the rope, he would always look down on me with disdain, and quickly remind me I was too little.

"But you could hold me up," I begged, but he would not relinquish his position as the official dinner bell ringer.

The dinner bell also had a secondary function. That was to alert the neighbors that help was needed. For example, if there was a fire, or someone was stricken ill, or maybe an elderly person had fallen and a family member needed help getting him up, then the dinner bell would be rung. But, since everyone in the Wiswell community tried to be self-sufficient, it would be highly unusual to hear the bell ring except at dinner-time. But I didn't know this at that time.

When the men came in to eat, they would wash their hands in the old dented aluminum wash pan, and then gather around the table. The women would "wait on" (serve) the men, before they, themselves, would eat.

Everyone was sated with the delicious food, and feeling a little sluggish, and since this time was the hottest part of the day, it was deemed too hot to go back into the fields for a couple hours. The men would go into the living room and lay down on the cool linoleum floors to rest and perhaps take a nap. Since much of the farm work required bending over, it was "back breaking" labor. Granddaddy especially complained of lumbago, and to ease his discomfort, he would take a straight-back chair, turn it backside up, tilted at an angle, on the floor, and place a pillow on it. Then he would sit on the floor and lean back on the chair, and soon would be snoring.

The women didn't need to rest, or so it was thought, as they had left the field early to cook dinner, and that was not considered work. So, they would wash the dishes and clean the kitchen. Then they would place the food left for supper onto the red and white checked oil cloth that covered the table, and spread a white cotton tablecloth over it. Then it would be time for the men and women to go back to the field.

There was no need to ring the dinner bell in the evening to announce supper, as everyone would work until it was almost too dark to see. There would be enough food intentionally prepared at noon to serve for supper, though a small fire might be started in the cook stove to heat one eye, so that cornbread patties could be fried on top of the stove. They were so good, along with some tasty buttermilk.

We had ordinary kerosene—we called it 'coal oil'—lamps. I wanted to light the wick, but was told I wasn't old enough to be trusted to strike the match or handle anything with fire. But I was old enough to clean the lamp globe, and of course I hated the mundane job of rubbing the glass chimney with old wadded up newspapers to remove the soot. When the lamps were lit, it seemed the room was flooded with light. But when compared to my grandparent's lamps, ours seemed to just be a weak yellow flickering light. Theirs was called the Aladdin Lamp, and had a round wick, that gave a powerful bright light. Mama complained that the light was so bright it hurt her eyes. Granddaddy said that the traveling salesman who sold it to him told him that if anyone could show him an oil lamp that would equal the Aladdin Lamp, the company would give them a reward of one-thousand dollars; the reward was never collected.

When I was about 8 years old, Granddaddy died. Granny and Aunt Margie continued to live alone in their home near us, and we visited back and forth often. One day Mama, Papa, and I were at their place helping them plant a garden.

Aunt Margie and Granny were wearing brand new bonnets, that Margie had recently made. They were so pretty, and I recognized they were made from the left-over material of Granny's new dress. The fabric had pink roses, which were her favorite flowers. The brims were heavily starch and ironed so they were very stiff. Their bonnets were kept in place by ribbons tied under their chins. The brims were pulled low over their foreheads to protect them from the sun. Delicate fair complexion was so much more desired than sun tanning, which everyone knew could lead to premature wrinkles.

"I had quite a scare last night," Aunt Margie said. "After supper I heard someone knock on the front door. Mother had already gone to bed, and I was afraid it may have appeared that I was there alone, but I answered it, anyway. And there stood a tramp.

"He was so dirty, soot all over him, maybe from riding the freight train or box cars. His clothes were ragged, and his hair and beard were long and unkept. When I saw him, I quickly reached up and hooked the screen door." She was frowning as she described him and looked as though she was recalling the distasteful sight he had presented.

"He carried his 'bindle' bunched up and tied to the end of a stick and slung over his shoulder. I guess he might have had a blanket in it since he would have been sleeping outside.

He said he knew he looked a fright, but he meant no harm. That he was just traveling the country and looking for a little work from time to time. Then he added that he was very hungry and asked if I might have some scraps left from supper. Now I was afraid to open the door, yet I know the Lord says we're to share anything we have with the less fortunate. Why, my favorite verses in the Bible are John 13: 35, 'By this all men will know that you are my disciples, if you love one another' and Matthew 25: 34-36 that says '…whatsoever you do to the least of these, my brothers, that you do unto me.'" She quoted these verses from memory, and then added, "That's to say nothing of what The Ten Commandments teaches us."

As an afterthought she said, "Somewhere in the Bible, I can't just turn to it right now, it says you might entertain angels unaware and that if anyone doesn't honor them by ministering to them, that they are to shake the dust off of their feet on to the door step and the house owner will be punished by the Lord."

Aunt Margie said that though she was frightened, she went back to the kitchen and found a large piece of corn bread, the only food left from supper. There was still some buttermilk in the jug, so she got a pint Mason jar out of the pantry and poured the buttermilk into it. "I sure didn't want to let him drink out of one of my glasses," she explained.

"When I went back to the door, I told him, 'you go back down the steps out yonder into the yard, and I'll just lay this food here on the porch and you can come back up and get it.' I did that and quickly hooked the door again. He said, 'much obliged, ma'am' and he sat down on the edge of the porch with his feet resting on the doorstep and began to gulp down the food. I noticed his shoes had holes in them and were laced with sea-grass strings.

"A few minutes later I peeked around and saw he had left the empty Mason jar on the porch and he was nowhere to be seen. But I'm telling you, I hardly slept a wink all night."

Mama and Papa commiserated with her about the frightening experience, but Mama told her she had done the right thing by listening to her Christian conscience.

Aunt Margie continued, "When I took my cream to market at Taylor Store this morning, I was telling Ed and Myrtle Morton about what happened. Ed thought it might be possible that the tramp was still in the neighborhood, so he said he was going to warn everybody to be on the alert."

I got tired of dropping the seeds in the rows, so I dumped the last handful at the end of the row and kicked the dirt over it so no one could see them. I hadn't realized that my transgression would be very obvious in a few days when the seeds sprouted, and a mass of black-eyed pea vines were found to be growing in one spot.

Then I slipped around the house to see if I could find one of Aunt Margie's kittens. I found the pretty orange one, and it let me pick it up. I stroked its back and it purred contentedly. I was going to ask Aunt Margie if I could take it home with me.

The chickens milled around the yard, pecking at insects or seeds in the grass. I went into the hen house and looked in all the nests and counted 12 eggs. That's exactly one dozen eggs, I thought, and was proud I knew that fact.

Granny's roses were blooming, and their fragrance filled the air. I decided I would pick a bouquet, but a thorn pricked my finger and I elected to forego that pleasure.

It was getting toward evening, and I was becoming bored. As I passed by Granny's dinner bell, I noticed the rope seemed to be a little longer than on our dinner bell. "I wonder if I can reach the rope," I thought. I went over to the bell. The rope was still just out of my reach. "But maybe if I stand on my tip toes, I can reach it." I tried it. Success! I grabbed the end of the rope and pulled mightily. The bell began to ring, loud and clear. So melodious! It was music to my ears. I was already thinking of how I would challenge my brother for the position of official dinner bell ringer. After a few rings, the rope slipped from my hands.

Just about this time Aunt Margie came running around the house toward me, Mama and Papa in close pursuit.

"Oh, you shouldn't have done that. When the neighbors hear the dinner bell at this time of day, they'll think we're in trouble here."

And the neighbors came. Some came on foot, rushing straightway through fields, as the crow flies, not taking time to go by the road. Others came on their horses, riding bare-back, not waiting to strap on the saddle. I could see the men still in their work clothes, some carrying rifles, the women in their aprons, as they crested the horizon, thinking they were answering a call of distress. They came from as far as the tolling of the bell could be heard. Many years later I would still be able to see this picture in my mind's eye.

Aunt Margie explained to them that the bell had been rung by accident, more or less, and apologized profusely. She even invited them in for a glass of lemonade or sweet tea, but everybody refused. Most of the responders took it all in good spirits; some even laughed, but I knew from Mama's expression that she was very displeased. And she confirmed this by saying, "Don't you know these neighbors are tired from working in the field all day? They were probably just sitting down to supper. And to have this big disruption is shameful. It's a disgrace."

When all the neighbors had gone back home, Aunt Margie told me to come sit in the swing on the front porch. She sat down beside me and put her arm around me. "I want to tell you a story," she said. "It's called *The Boy Who Cried Wolf.*"

And she told me that once upon a time there was a little boy whose job was to watch over and protect his family's sheep, to keep them safe from the wolves who roamed the hills.

I imagined seeing the white, curly wool creatures eating the green grass on the hillside. Since my Uncle Cratic and Aunt Lizzie had sheep, and I had even been present during shearing time, I knew how soft and fluffy they were.

She continued to tell me about the little boy who tended the sheep. I interrupted her to tell her that I knew he was called a shepherd. "He got tired of being in the field with no one but the sheep to keep him company. But his family really trusted him to care for the sheep. So, they left him alone. Then he decided if he cried 'Wolf!' real loud, maybe someone would come and stay with him awhile. So, he did cry 'Wolf!' and some of the villagers came running but found there had not been a wolf. The boy laughed at them for falling for his ruse. This happened another 2 or 3 times, and the villagers came. And the boy laughed and laughed.

"Finally, the wolf really did come, and the boy cried 'Wolf! Wolf! Please come and help me. The wolf is killing the sheep.' But no one believed him, and no one came when he really needed help.

"So, just like the villagers in that story, our neighbors heard the bell ring out and as it was not dinner time, they thought it was a call for help. This was true especially because they knew that there had been a tramp at my house last night."

"And my ringing the dinner bell was like the boy crying wolf?" I asked. "I didn't mean to make everyone come. I was so excited to see I had grown enough to reach the rope on the dinner bell! I won't ever do it again," I promised.

Aunt Margie pulled me into her lap and hugged me tight. "You didn't know that would happen; but now you do. So, let that be a lesson to you."

Mama, however, elected a different method of teaching me a lesson. It involved breaking off a switch from the peach tree. Peach tree switches are very pliable and would cling and sting when applied to my legs or backside. A little whipping with a peach tree switch was called making "peach tree tea."

But I did learn a lesson; something that would become a guiding force throughout my life. And that is: ***You can't un-ring the bell!***

The Cliques

I was a skinny little girl when I started to school. Skinny, with knobby knees. And tall. I heard grownups discuss the possibility that I might grow up to be as tall as my Aunt Margie, who measured six feet exactly. And from the worried tone of their voices I surmised that would not be a good thing. But I had one thing going for me. I had the most beautiful long platinum blonde hair. My older sisters kept my hair brushed and curled, but when they graduated and went to Detroit to work, Mama put my hair in pigtails, which I hated with a passion and still detest today.

At school, we lined up for all occasions, alphabetically. My last name was Wilkerson, so I was usually in the back of the line, except on occasion when the teacher, being inventive, would use the alphabet backwards, to even things out. When she did this she always said, "And the first shall be last." She was the same teacher who admonished us to study for a test, by predicting that otherwise there will be weeping and wailing and gnashing of teeth.

Standing in line, I was taller than Johnny West, who's name also began with a W, and, therefore was always next to me. It would have surprised me then if I had known that Johnny (who soon insisted on being just called John) would grow up to be 6 feet 5 inches tall, play college basketball, and have a career as a coach. I would only be 5 feet 5 inches.

There were definitely little cliques in my class. The upper echelon was ruled by a girl named Gloria. She, her brother Sammie, and their parents lived with their grandparents almost directly across the road from the school.

Gloria had nicer clothes than the other kids, her cigar box was decorated prettily, and chock full of colors. She had a huge jar of paste, with a little brush for applying it. And she even had a slick leaf tablet from her very first day of school, while the rest of us had rough leaf tablets, with pictures of an Indian Chief on the red front covers. One day Gloria came to school wearing new cowboy boots. This elevated her status to the point that she no longer deigned to carry her own books, but delegated this chore to Imogene, who was barely on the periphery of that clique, but felt honored to oblige, as she looked longingly at the boots.

Ruth Flowers was definitely on the lowest rung of the social ladder. Her clothes were worn and ill fitting, but worst of all she wore thick heavy brown long cotton stockings, the only one in the class to do so. And to make things worse she used the red rubber bands utilized in canning with Mason jars, as garters to hold the stockings up.

Robbie Jo was her own clique; she didn't ride the school bus, but rather her mother drove her to school. Upon arrival she would lean over and give her mother a kiss, jump out of the car and skip happily to her classroom. She was so smart she was allowed to skip a grade, which put her in my classroom. She was also very talented and was given many opportunities by her doting parents. Among those were her dance lessons and she seemed to specialize in tap dancing.

Our school offered many social activities for the whole community to come for entertainment, cake walks, ice cream suppers, and especially the Junior and Senior Class plays. During intermission, the big heavy red velvet curtains would open up, and there on the stage stood Robbie Jo. She would perform her tap dance routine. Everyone was mesmerized by her performances, or I know I was. I was so envious of her real tap shoes, black patent leather with a strap shaped like a bow, and the sound they made as she danced on the wooden floor of the stage. And her socks were so white, and turned down like cuffs, which were edged with lace; we called them anklets. I idolized her and memorized her every move. Afterwards, I would come home and entertain my dog. I imitated what I saw Robbie Jo do; I was sure I could "Shuffle off to Buffalo" as well as she could!

And then there was Ann, who had a twin brother. They even had twin-sounding names, Ann and Dan. They had several brothers and sisters, most of whom were older than Ann, and they always took care of her if she needed anything.

In my first couple of years at Lynn Grove School, everyone carried their lunches. Peanut butter, deviled ham, potted meat, or cheese sandwiches were the daily fare. One girl in my class, Marie Spann, brought tasty sausage and biscuits, and her mother, Mrs. Altie, made chocolate fried pies for Marie. Oh, those chocolate fried pies! Though futile, I attempted to trade her out of one of those pies. I had been under the impression that fried pies must consist of apple, peach, or maybe cherry. But I was sure chocolate would have been so much more delectable. I never found out.

Instead of packing our lunches in paper bags, (and none of us had lunch boxes) Mama folded up pages from the newspaper to resemble a pocket, a true artistic achievement I was sure, and then stuffed the food items wrapped in wax paper, inside.

A year or two later a new cafeteria was added to our school. Our Principal, Mr. Buron "Boots" Jeffery, told Mama I was to receive free lunches, not based on income level but because I was so underweight, which saved them the 16 ½ cents charged for each meal. Apparently, the government subsidized the cost of the meals and large quantities of food arrived at the lunchroom every day, including dried Great Northern beans by the huge bag full, and they were served frequently. The two cooks, one of whom was Gloria's grandmother, arrived early each morning to put the beans on to cook. The beans required a long time to cook, and sometimes they were served before they were completely cooked, which meant biting into them yielded a crunchy unpleasant taste. Cabbage was shredded and made into Cole slaw and served on the same plate where all the food ran together. Cabbage and beans. What could be the results of kids eating these two vegetables, and then being shut up in a stuffy classroom, especially in the hot summertime? I received free meals but that didn't mean I had to eat them.

But then one day there was something really special! We were each given a homemade sugar cookie. It tasted so good, almost as good as the ones my grandmother made with molasses, which she called tea cakes. I took little nibbles of my cookie, to make it last longer. Then I saw Gloria and her brother, Sammie, go up to the lunch counter, where their grandmother gave them each another cookie. "Oh seconds!" I thought. I wolfed down the rest of my remaining cookie, presented myself at the lunch counter to request my second cookie, only to find that the privilege of a bonus cookie did not extend to non-relatives.

My First Hamburger

Word had gotten around the first-grade classroom that we were going to be served hamburgers in the lunchroom soon. I hoped it would take the place of the weekly under-cooked white "soup beans" and Cole slaw Day.

Joette and I knew what hamburgers were, but we had not ever eaten one. Ronald Crouch had opened a little diner in downtown Lynn Grove, and when we were on the "late bus" schedule, we often went there to watch the more affluent students partake of his delicacies. Betty Underwood and Patricia Morton would often saunter into the diner and find their places on the red plastic stools that lined up at the counter, which were the only seating in the place. There were mis-matched salt and pepper shakers and little glass cannisters of sugar that streamed out of the tiny opening on top when turned upside down, placed at intervals along the counter. I noticed there were crumbled-up crackers inside the sugar jars, which I was told kept the sugar from lumping. Beside the sugar jars, shiny chrome napkin dispensers were handy.

Since Joette and I were not paying customers we merely stood in the corner and watched. But to see Betty and Patricia nonchalantly order hamburgers, and see Ronald cook them up on the grill behind the counter, to say nothing of getting to savor the delicious aroma, was certainly worth the little trek to Ronald's Diner, and then back to the school house in time to catch the bus on its second run.

Ronald not only served hamburgers, but also hotdogs, though he only had hamburger buns. No problem. Hot dogs were simply sliced to fit the round bun. Hotdogs were 15 cents, while hamburgers were a whole 20 cents. The huge glass bottles of Coca-Colas were another nickel each. To our amazement, sometimes Betty and Patricia did not finish their entire hamburgers, leaving morsels on their plates. We guessed they'd never heard about all the starving children in China. The ones I was so familiar with. After eating, they always took napkins and daintily wiped just the corners of their mouths. I admired them so much and wanted to be just like them.

Here it was Thursday again. And I had been peeking through the door to the lunch room during recess to determine if the rumor that hamburgers were to be served today was true. But I could only see Gloria's grandmother and Mrs. Ginny Lou's backs, as they hovered over the cook stove, with their massive white aprons wrapped around their entire dresses and their hair covered by hairnets. And yes, it was true. Hamburger Day had finally arrived in the Lynn Grove High School lunchroom.

We were each given our plate where a hamburger patty was placed between two slices of white bread. Two slivers of dill pickles and a streak of mustard adorned the burger. I had noticed that Ronald had put pickles, mustard, onions, and even red tomato ketchup on the hamburgers he served at the diner, and that he had mayonnaise for those more discerning patrons who requested it.

Nevertheless, this, my first hamburger, was the most delicious thing I had ever tasted. At home we only had fried chicken, country ham, pork tenderloin, or best of all, country backbones. Or maybe there would be pork sausage patties or crisp bacon. And always fresh vegetables in season, or home canned, or later, frozen, when we could rent a freezer locker in town, and eventually when the availability of electricity allowed us to have our own "deep freeze". But we had never had anything as extravagant as a hamburger.

That night at supper time I regaled everybody with a description of my gourmet experience. "Oh, that sounds so good," Mama said, and she winked at Papa, as she passed the big bowl of home-grown English peas with tiny new potatoes cooked together. She placed a serving of tender pot roast on my plate, as I looked with scorn at my supper. I felt so sorry for Mama and Papa because they had not experienced the ultimate in dining pleasure, as I most certainly had.

At last it was Thursday again. And as hoped for, hamburgers were served again. As I took my plate to the big long table and stepped over the picnic bench style seat, I began to feel pangs of guilt. Here I had this big hamburger, while at home Mama was probably eating an old pork chop or maybe left-over chicken and dumplings. Besides I wasn't sure I had done a good job of describing the tantalizing attributes of my epicurean delight last night. They had not seemed unduly impressed, as I had expected they would. Perhaps they needed to see with their own eyes.

So, what to do? "I know," I thought. "I'll take this hamburger to Mama." It was very tempting to eat it, but no, I would be the good daughter and take it home to Mama. I didn't have a bag or a box; or even a newspaper to wrap it in, and there was no tin foil available to me. (I guess plastic wrap had not been invented). So, not to be outdone, I simply put the hamburger, uncovered, on top of my stack of books.

It continued to set on top of my books in my cubbyhole against the wall until time to go home. I gathered up my books, hamburger still in place, and carried it thusly on the school bus all the way home. The other kids were very curious as to why my hamburger was being carried on top of my books, and I had to shoo them away to keep them from touching it. There were times when the sandwich almost slid off but I managed to retrieve it before it hit the floor. By now it began to look a little worse for wear; the bread appeared to be getting slightly dried out but it still smelled delicious.

When I entered our house I called out, "Mama, Mama!" I couldn't wait for her to see the treasure I had brought her. The guilt I had felt had abated, and I longed to see her eyes light up as she received my gift.

I'll always remember what she said when she saw my offering. "Oh Honey, you should not have brought that to me. You should have eaten it yourself."

So, I did!

Papa's First (and Last) Home-Made Biscuits

In the early 1940's the population of Wiswell and surrounding areas grew sparse; first, because so many young men were drafted or volunteered for the military, but also as so many residents moved to Detroit to work in the defense plants. Brent Atkins drove the Brooks Bus and kept the road hot, transporting those who were eagerly hoping to earn some money, after being victims of the Great Depression for so long. My sisters, Rebecca and Iva Nel, who had recently graduated high school, announced that they wanted to go to seek work in Detroit. Papa said that they could go, but asked them to wait until the Fall, as he needed their help in getting the crops harvested.

When they arrived in Detroit, they stayed with friends, Bill and Norette Hill, who had emigrated from Wiswell the year before. Rebecca found work in a plant manufacturing parts for B-29's, which were the Super Fortress bombers, but Iva Nel, who was only 17 years old, had to settle for a job in a dime store. They continued living with the Hill's, paying $7 per week for room and board until they got their first pay checks; then they rented a tiny apartment.

They had been gone almost a year, and we missed them terribly; I especially did, as I had been their "doll" receiving so much attention. I begged to go see them, and Mama began to consider making the trip by bus. "Maybe we had better go now, because if the gas shortage gets much worse the bus may stop running," she said.

She went to see my principal, Mr. Buron "Boots" Jeffery, and got permission to take me out of school for a few days. She picked up my homework assignments from my second-grade teacher; then we packed our bags and away we went.

We were welcomed to headquarter our visit at Bill and Norette Hill's house, as my sisters' apartment was too small to accommodate overnight guests. But we all got together as soon as the girls got off work in the evenings.

One day a little boy, who lived next door, Glenn Eaker, who was about my age, came, with his mother to visit. They had formerly lived close to the Hill family in Wiswell, and after coming to Detroit they had managed to rent a house next door to them, so their close relationship remained intact.

"I have a new card game," Glenn bragged. And he held up a brand-new deck of playing cards. "It's called 'Hearts'. Me and my buddy play it all the time." He jutted his chin out, trying to look superior, and then added "I'm getting really good at it. I think I'm about ready to 'shoot the moon.'"

"Let me see them," I begged.

"No, they're mine. Girls don't know how to play."

"I know how," I lied.

"No, you don't."

"I've played it lots of times," I lied, again.

And I reached out for the cards. He jerked them out of my reach which, of course, forced me to lunge forward to grab them. Suddenly he let out a blood curdling scream and jumped up, cards flying everywhere! While he was distracted, I was scrambling trying to pick up the loose cards. He was jumping about and pointing towards his upper arm where a tiny trickle of blood was running down. In the melee I had bumped his arm at the site of his recent smallpox vaccination, and the scab had come off.

Mama was so embarrassed and humiliated when she saw what I had done. She said, "Everywhere she goes she just seems to wreak havoc."

I had no idea what havoc was, or how I went about wreaking it, but to hear Mama's fancy words describing my exploits, I was certain it was a pretty grand achievement, and I felt somewhat important.

I was commanded to apologize, forthwith, and as if such an apology wasn't enough, she forced me to kiss his cheek. He was mortified! The kiss was far more painful than the physical injury.

That night, when my sisters came home from work, I heard Mama recount the day's activities to them. She started by saying, "Well, Linda Fay sure showed out today!"

Before leaving home, Mama had prepared a lot of food for Papa and the boys. But since Papa was used to having Mama's delicious fluffy biscuits every morning, the toast from "store-boughten" bread, referred to as 'light bread' was just not sufficient. His favorite breakfast was sausage patties and eggs, with biscuits, finished off with home churned butter and molasses and more biscuits!

After a day or two he began to think, "Well how hard can it be to make biscuits? Jewel makes them every day." So, he got out her bread board. It was a scooped out bowl-shaped container made of oak, and polished to a fine shine. He had made it himself and had given it to his new bride when they were first married.

He started a good fire in the wood burning cook stove and turned his attention to the task at hand. He knew Mama put the flour in the bread board first. He knew there was supposed to be baking soda, salt, and baking powder added, but how much?

"I'll try a spoonful of each," he thought. He knew the lard would make the biscuits flaky, "so I'll add a right smart of lard, and then some butter milk." He was squeezing all the ingredients together with his hands, as he had seen Mama do.

Just then someone knocked on the front door. "Who could that be?" he wondered. Any of the neighbors would have just walked in, calling out loudly to announce their arrival. The door was never locked. Indeed, we would have been hard pressed to even find a key. The knocking became louder and more insistent. With biscuit dough up to his elbows, he went to answer the door. And there, backed up to the front door, was a terrifying sight that he would never forget! There was a long black hearse and an undertaker from J. H. Churchill Funeral Home standing at the door. Papa said he thought his heart would stop. He was certain there had been an accident and that Mama and I had been killed. At that time, it was common practice to bring the body of the deceased to the home for viewing and visitation, and maybe the funeral service, followed by the trip to the cemetery for burial.

Then the undertaker spoke: "Is this the home of Mr. Earnest Erwin? We had a call that he has been killed in a farm accident, and I'm here to pick up his body." Papa informed him that he was at the wrong house; that the Erwin house was the next one on the left on up the road.

Mr. Erwin had fallen off the back of a wagon load of hay bales, and hit his head on the frozen ground and was killed. Papa said his great relief at learning his wife and young daughter were okay was greatly diminished by realizing his beloved neighbor was killed in such a tragic accident. Mama and Papa had been neighbors of the Erwin's ever since they had been married, and had relied on them, as they were older and wiser, for guidance and advice in farming, gardening, and child rearing.

One thing for certain, his biscuits were no longer of any importance. In fact, the dough found its way into the pigs' slop bucket, which was probably an appropriate place for it anyway.

Papa was never a very demonstrative, openly affectionate person. When he told us of this terrible incident, he still did not come right out and say he loved us. But that was okay. We all knew he did.

Poplin, of the "Turnip Green Patch Story"

When Poplin discovered that the man whom she thought she was marrying had suddenly and without warning married another woman, she was shocked. To make matters worse, she was dressed in her wedding gown waiting for him to pick her up so they could elope when she was told of this devastating news. He had eloped, but not with her. She realized that her hopes and dreams of a happy marriage with the man who had so freely professed love for her, was hopeless, as he now belonged to someone else.

The news of her "condition" spread like wildfire. An illegitimate child on the way. Such a disgrace. Consequently, she was kept cloistered in her home, where her mother frequently reminded her of the shame she had brought on her family's name. No one seemed to put the blame on her lover, but assumed she had seduced him.

"You might as well wear a scarlet 'A' on your forehead, like that adulteress did, in that book that Pastor Hamlin preached against Sunday morning; that sinful book, that he forbade anyone to read. He was looking straight at you!" Poplin could only bow her head in shame, as her mother continued her tirade. "I think you'll stay away from church from now on, Poplin Smith. And when the peddling wagon comes, you stay in the house out of sight; I'll do the trading. In fact, since you're already beginning to show, you can just stay in the house, altogether."

Poplin had gone to Miss Sadie, the local midwife, early on, and had been given an approximate date for her confinement. The midwife had been kindly, and in a reassuring tone of voice said, "Honey, you're not the first, and no doubt you'll not be the last," as she gave her a gentle pat on the back.

Her mother had bought a length of flannel material from the peddler and had made two little gowns for the expected baby, as well as cut narrows strips of cloth to serve as a belly band. "You'll need to put this band on around the belly to hold its navel in, so it won't stick out and look ugly, and maybe even cause a hernia." She had also made a couple of diapers and secured two safety pins in readiness for the baby.

After Poplin went to bed that night, she laid her hand gently on her abdomen, and whispered loving words to her baby. "I'll always take care of you, sweet Carrie," because she believed—and wished—with all her heart that her baby would be a girl. This became a nightly ritual, and was always her last thoughts as she lulled herself to a peaceful sleep.

After a while her mother began to reconcile herself to the inevitable, and had calmed down, somewhat. Some afternoons she and Poplin would take glasses of lemonade and sit on the front porch. They were acutely aware that neighbors, formerly friendly, ignored them as they walked by. The mothers in the group would caution their daughters to look the other way. It was as if viewing an unwed pregnant woman might be contagious.

They certainly did not want to wave at her, or heaven forbid, speak to her, as this might be construed as approving of, or at least accepting, the illegitimate pregnancy.

A couple of weeks prior to her due date she began to experience an uncomfortable cramping sensation, but she tried to ignore it, as she tossed and turned, trying to find a comfortable position in bed. "Not time yet," she thought, attempting to disregard her discomfort. But the pains continued, so she got up and rekindled the fire in the fireplace, and started the early morning chores. But the tightening of her womb intensified and the contractions were coming at more frequent intervals and were accompanied with excruciating pain. She finally called out to her mother. They determined it was probably her time, though a little earlier than the midwife had said. "Maybe you're farther along than you thought," suggested her mother. "You've always been bigger than the dates would seem." But Poplin was sure of the conception date, but said nothing to refer to that time.

And so it was that on this very cold February morning, her mother hitched up her horse to the buggy, and went to get the midwife. When she arrived, she hurried down from the buggy and knocked on the door. Despite her anger at Poplin she was feeling anxious about leaving her alone. She knocked again, and a little boy in a flannel nightshirt and tousled blonde curls opened the door. But he opened it only slightly, not wanting to add the cold outside air to the cold room inside.

"Mama's not here," he volunteered, not waiting for a question. "She's gone to deliver a baby. Don't know where. Been gone all night. Said not to worry, because where ever she is when she gets through, she might just lay down there and sleep awhile. Guess you'll need to go get the doctor." And he shut the door.

On her way back home, as the first few snowflakes were falling, Mrs. Smith stopped at the first farmhouse she came to. She wasn't sure who lived there. When the lady came to the door, Mrs. Smith told her of her predicament.

"I came to get the midwife, but she's away on another case. My daughter is at home in labor and is alone. I need to get back home to see after her." The woman was looking at her, stone faced. "Can I ask if the man of the house would please ride over to Dr. Barkley's and fetch him for the delivery?"

"Aren't you that woman whose daughter is having a baby out of wedlock?" Not waiting for an answer, she continued to express her opinion. "Don't know if the doctor will come out for a case like that. Wait here. I'll go ask my husband if he will go." With much indignant grumbling for being called upon to participate in such a shameful activity, he finally agreed to go.

Mrs. Smith hurried home to find Poplin writhing in pain. She began to wring her hands with concern, and frequently looked out the window for the appearance of the doctor.

When Dr. Barkley arrived in his own buggy, enshrouded in multiple layers of lamb's wool blankets, he was in a foul mood.

"I don't appreciate being called out in such bad weather," he said as he went to warm himself at the blazing fireplace. "It would be bad enough to come out for somebody who is somebody, but to come out to deliver a bastard that'll never amount to anything is against my principles!"

He sat his black medical bag on a near-by chair. "Get me a pan of warm water Mrs. Smith," he ordered, and she emptied the tea kettle into the wash basin and brought it to him. Then turning to Poplin, he pulled the bed covers back and started to examine her.

"Oh, please wait till this pain is over," she begged.

"Then there'll just be another. Besides I can tell more about what's happening during a pain."

"Please. Please don't be so rough. You're hurting me." Then, turning her head to the wall, she added, to no one in particular, "I'm so sorry. I'm so sorry." Her pleas were ignored as the doctor carried out the examination.

"I got here just in time. She's ready to start pushing," he said. And then turning to Mrs. Smith asked, "Do you have a step stool anywhere?" She brought the step stool from a nearby closet. "Put it there by the kitchen table." He brought his black bag and placed it in a nearby chair. He laid out some ominous-looking instruments.

To Poplin he said, "Now get up and step on that stool and climb up on the kitchen table and lay down. I need you on a flat surface, not buried up in that feather bed, and I'm sure not going to break my back bending over this low bed.

"Hold her legs apart, Mrs. Smith"

"I can't do this," screamed Poplin "I've got to get out of here. Just let me run away," and she struggled to get up.

Dr. Barkley grabbed her hair and jerked her back in a supine position, and not missing an opportunity to reprimand her said, "You should have thought of this when you were out having fun."

Finally, a little baby, all red and squalling, was delivered. "Is my baby alright?" asked Poplin? "I want to see her. Let me see my sweet Carrie. Mama, let me hold her"

"It's a boy," her mother responded. "He looks like he's okay; just small."

The cord was tied and cut. He was quickly wrapped in a quilt and taken to the hearth by the fire. He continued to cry at the top of his lungs. Dr. Barkley delivered the afterbirth, which was added to the logs in the fireplace. The odor of burning flesh permeated the room. Mrs. Smith rolled up some cotton and wrapped it with a clean rag, making a pad, and placed it on Poplin to absorb the bleeding.

"You can get up off the table now and get back in your bed." Then addressing Mrs. Smith, he said, "Having a baby this easy may make her more likely to repeat such a thing again. Don't call me if she gets in trouble again, for I won't be coming a second time."

As he went out the door he said, "Not only did I have to get up out of my good warm bed, but I haven't even had my breakfast yet. I'll be expecting you to come by and pay my bill in a day or two. If you need anything else, go get the midwife."

Poplin gratefully crawled back into her bed. "But Mama, I still hurt," she cried.

"That's just after-pains. That's normal. Hush up, while I tend to the young 'un. What kind of name are you going to give him? Make sure it's not a family name, or the same as anyone around here, as we don't want anyone speculating as to who the daddy is."

"But Mama, the pains are as bad as ever and getting worse. They just won't stop!" she wailed. She tossed and turned but her Mama had become engrossed in caring for the new baby which in spite of herself, she was holding tenderly. The baby had responded by sucking on his tiny fist. She held up one of the new little gowns to the fire to warm before pulling it on over the baby's head. She was folding a diaper to put on the baby and was holding the safety pin in her mouth in readiness to secure it, but then she heard Poplin scream.

"Mama. Something's coming out of me. Do something."

"Oh, it's probably a blood clot. I've heard of that happening after a baby is born. Or maybe it's a piece off of the afterbirth that tore loose. You would know it would be after the doctor is gone." She laid the baby back in the quilt, turned back the bedcovers to see a little baby's head protruding, and with an involuntary push from Poplin, the body quickly followed.

"My Lord. It's twins. And it's another boy" She looked around to find something to tie the cord, and then she pulled a shoestring from her shoe and tied the cord. Then she grabbed some scissors from the mending basket on the dresser and cut the cord. Soon a second afterbirth was added to the fire. She wrapped both boys in the quilt and laid them near the fireplace, until she brought an empty dresser drawer to serve as their bed.

"Lucky they don't look alike, or otherwise I wouldn't remember which one was born first," her mother said. "But they look so different from each other it'll be easy to tell them apart." Both babies were quite vigorous, kicking, and flailing their arms. "It's a good thing I made two little gowns."

After a while her mother helped Poplin express some breast first-milk into a spoon, and then, with a medicine dropper, dribbled a taste into each baby's mouth. When offered the breast each baby latched on and nursed voraciously. With one baby cradled in each arm, the disappointment of not getting the longed-for Baby Carrie soon dissipated. And like millions of new mothers before and after her, the memory of the pain receded, replaced with the joy of motherhood. Even the shame she had felt for months was secondary to her new-found elation, as she gazed at the perfect babies.

"I've decided on names," Poplin said. "The one with the head full of hair will be named William; the other, with just a little fuzz on his head is Walter."

Soon afterwards the news of surprise twins traveled the neighborhood, and a few of the closest neighbors came to visit. Mrs. Lou Belle Sanders brought an arm load of used baby clothes, and well-worn diapers, which were gladly received. Since she was a much-respected member of the community, her act of kindness was likely to be followed by others in the neighborhood. Another neighbor told Mrs. Smith she hoped Poplin would do her washing and ironing for her when she was able, as that would bring in a little extra income for her.

When spring came, they would plant an even bigger garden, and can and dry food, as they always did, but in larger quantities. Both Poplin and her mother found themselves looking forward to the future.

The boys grew fast and were healthy. One day in the late Spring, when they were a little over two years old, they were having great fun playing in the front yard. They were barefoot, and shirtless, so that their upper bodies were brown as a nut. Their hair had grown so that now both boys had dark ringlets that covered their heads. They both had azure blue eyes that sparkled when they laughed. They were happy boys, playing with each other and not prone to mischief, not requiring correcting by their mother or grandmother. They had grown to look more alike. Everyone said they must be identical. Poplin sat in a rocker on the front porch, watching them play, while patching the knees of a little pair of bib overalls.

One of the boys saw a dandelion growing by the mailbox, and he went over and picked it. He ran to his mother and proudly held it out to her. "For you, Mama. For you."

"Oh, what a beautiful flower. Thank you, Will"

Seeing what his brother had done, Walter began to search the yard for a similar prize. Unable to find another flower, he pulled up a little fistful of grass, and ran to offer it to his mother. His gift was received with equal enthusiasm.

A horse and buggy were coming up their drive, as signaled by a cloud of dust stirred up from the movement of the horses' hooves. It stopped in the front yard. The boys had quit their play and were watching intently as the man got down from the buggy. Poplin could see him too. "Why it's Thomas," she thought. The woman with him stayed in the buggy, looking straight ahead.

"Hello, Poplin," Thomas began. "You have some fine-looking boys here."

"Yes," Poplin agreed.

Coming straight to the point, he said, "I have an offer to make to you that would be to everyone's advantage; especially these boys here." He took his hat off and stepped closer to the porch. He looked up at Poplin, and she noticed his sky-blue eyes, which had been one of the things about him that had caused her to fall in love with him.

"My wife hasn't been able to conceive, and well, she isn't getting any younger." (Poplin had heard she was older than Thomas.) "She has agreed that we could take these two boys off your hands, and that would be a load off your shoulder." He laughed and added, "That would be TWO loads off your shoulders."

When she did not respond to his joviality, he more seriously added, "I'm in a good position to adopt them. (He never alluded to the paternity of the boys.) I can see that they get the things they need." He glanced at the overalls Poplin was patching. "Good clothes, and I can even send them to school when they're old enough" After a moment's pause, he added," I could even give you a little money, so you don't have to wash other people's dirty clothes."

Poplin looked unflinchingly straight into his blue eyes and said, "No, thank you. They're not for sale. They are mine," stressing the word 'mine'. "We are making it just fine."

"Well at least think about it. You don't have to make up your mind right now."

"I don't have to think about it at all," she countered.

"You're making a big mistake. You had better reconsider," he said in a threatening tone of voice.

She got up from her chair, and called, "William, Walter, come on in. It's almost supper time." As the boys joined her on the porch, and she opened the door to go in, she turned back to Thomas and said, "I'll thank you to leave now."

"Who was that, Mama?' both boys asked simultaneously.

"Who? Why that was nobody." And taking each of their little hands in her own, they went into the house.

Without looking back, she firmly shut the door.

The Step Mothers

When my mother, Jewel was five years old her mother died. Her brother, Lynn was three, and sister Amy was just a baby. At that time the deceased, after embalming, was usually returned from the mortuary to the home, where visitation, and maybe the funeral would be held. And such was the case when her mother, Rebecca Priscilla Sanders Adams died after a brief illness.

Jewel said she remembered when they brought the open casket into the living room, she pushed a chair up next to it and crawled up, looked over and saw her mother lying there. She began to cry, and begged to sleep with her mother. Her uncle lifted her down from the chair, and said, "You can't sleep with her tonight, Jewel."

Then she heard a woman say to another woman, "Take those earrings out of Becky's ears. Don't bury them with her, for they are pure gold."

When it was getting late most of the visitors left, except a man and his wife who volunteered to sit up all night with the deceased. This was a custom perhaps started as a pagan ritual, to protect the soul from evil spirits, but it was done now as a show of respect for the person who had passed and courtesy toward the family.

At the funeral, Jewel heard people saying, "How is Dave going to take care of these three little ones? His mother isn't well, so she can't be much help."

It was hard to imagine a young farmer, a widower, with three young children trying to keep his family together. At five years of age, Jewel was trying to take care of the other two children, while her Daddy worked in the fields. One day she found a little lard bucket. She put some potatoes in it, added some water, and placed it on the heating stove to cook. When her Daddy came to the house, she proudly showed him her contribution to dinner.

When that story was told to me many years later, she said, "Amazingly, he actually ate those potatoes. They must have been pitiful, but I'll always remember that he said, 'These are the best potatoes I ever tasted' for he was always so positive and encouraging."

One evening when Jewel was about six years old, a doctor who lived around Kirksey came to their house in his nice new buggy. Jewel looked out the living room window and could see the beautiful red horse hooked to the buggy. The reins had been wrapped around the limb of the oak tree that stood near the front door. The window faced the west and the sun was going down. The entire western sky was blood red. Her Daddy liked to see a red sunset. "That means a fair day tomorrow. I can get lots of work done," he always said.

The doctor was invited in. He had on a black suit and white shirt. His hair was salt and pepper, but his moustache was all gray. He took his black hat off and he looked around the living room with its sparse furnishings. Then he said he wanted to speak to her Daddy.

"Daddy said 'Jewel, you take Lynn and Amy into the kitchen.' It was like he didn't want us children to hear their conversation.

"Lynn and Amy went right along with me, as they always did what I asked," Jewel said, when she related her memories years later. "Looking back, I think they had transferred their love meant to go to a mother to me, even as young as I was. We were in the kitchen but I could hear what was being said. The doctor was speaking.

'Mr. Dave, my wife and I have not been blessed with children. That has been the biggest disappointment in our lives. We would love to adopt your oldest little girl, Jewel.' Daddy didn't say anything. Then the doctor spoke again. 'My wife saw her at school, and she has her heart set on bringing her to our home.' There was still silence.

"Then he went on to enumerate all of the advantages they could give me. There would be pretty clothes, nourishing food, a good education. I would be so well cared for, and loved deeply.

"I was petrified. Was I about to leave my Daddy and my home? Well I can tell you it was the happiest day of my life, before or since, when I heard my Daddy say, 'Oh no sir. Thank you kindly for the offer, but I could never part with my little girl,' and that meant I would get to stay at home with my little brother and sister."

Probably more by necessity than any other reason, Dave married again, to a woman named Annie Cobb. To this union there were three children born. There were two little girls, and then a little boy, Burie, who died in infancy.

Unfortunately, this woman was unhealthy physically and mentally. She was the epitome of the wicked step mother. Neighbors attested to the unbelievable acts of cruelty aimed at the three older children, some of them life threatening. Unfortunately, there was no intervention on behalf of the children because it was widely believed that it was up to the parents to discipline their children, including meting out punishment as they saw fit.

Jewel now had to take on the complete care of her two new step sisters, Omie and Elna, as well as still caring for Lynn and Amy. She also had to do most of the household chores. After the work was done, the step-mother often put Jewel, Lynn, and Amy, but not her own children, outside, even in cold or rainy weather, and refuse to let them come inside for hours. Once she sent Lynn to the root cellar to get a cup of brown sugar. When he brought it to her, she made him open his mouth so she could make sure he hadn't eaten any.

At one point, Annie Cobb became ill. Some members of her family came to take her to their home for recuperation. She refused to get out of bed, so her father and brothers loaded her, bed and all, onto the farm wagon being pulled with two mules. Jewel watched, with great joy, as the wagon traveled down the road, and finally disappeared out of sight. It wasn't very long until they brought her back.

Eventually she died. A few years later, Dave told the children that he was going to marry again. By now, Jewel was sixteen years old.

"I decided I would never again be treated the way that my last step-mother treated me," Jewel said. "I knew there was no work available for a sixteen-year-old girl, but I would do something, anything. Perhaps work in someone's home, take care of their children just for room and board. I would only ask to let me live there and get out of my situation.

"But when I met Mary Black, the woman who was to be my second step mother, I was pleasantly surprised. No, not just surprised, shocked, that was more like it. She was a kind, loving woman, the antitheses of her predecessor. She took on the maternal role for all of Daddy's five children. We were happy to accept her offer to call her Mother."

Again, there were three babies born, Virginia and J.D. who were vigorous and grew well and strong. Then last, there was little Alec Ralph, who died in his second summer, as so many children did at that age back then. It was believed that death at that age was due to eating fresh vegetables from the garden, as apparently the digestive system was too immature to process digestion. Little Alec Ralph had played in the garden while his sisters picked English peas. They did not notice that he was eating some peas straight from the pods. Everyone was convinced that was the cause of his demise. As a souvenir, Jewel kept the little certificate that showed Alec Ralph was recognized as being a member of the Cradle Roll at Sinking Spring Baptist Church. His short life had brought much love and joy to the Adams' household.

It was such a sad day when Mary died of consumption, later called tuberculosis, which was the cause of death listed on many death certificates in those days.

It was quite a coincidence as Dave's first wife, Rebecca Sanders' death occurred on March 2. It happened to also be March 2, several years later when Annie Cobb left this world. But Mary Black didn't die until March 3.

Jewel continued to live at home and care for the children. Amy, who was considered extraordinarily beautiful, was an outgoing popular young lady. She excelled in her school work and was a star basketball player at her two-room school, South Howard. She was proud of her basketball uniform, though it took some convincing to get her father to agree to let her wear the navy blue long pants, which really looked like a split long skirt, that had elastic around the bottom of each leg. The blouse was white, with a collar patterned after a navy uniform, and was really the style of the day. Finishing the outfit was a navy blue silk scarf tied around the neck of the blouse, with the long ends laying across the bodice in front, also in navy uniform fashion. Mother had just cut Amy's hair in the latest bob, which would become the hair-do symbolic of the upcoming Roaring '20's.

In 1918 the great Spanish Flu pandemic hit the entire country, taking the life of dear sweet Amy, at the age of nineteen years. She had been engaged to be married soon. Jewel grieved her whole life because Amy said she had called for her all night when she got sick, but Jewel didn't hear her. People said it seemed strange that everyone in the family was together at home, but only Amy was chosen by the Death Angel. Jewel's fiancé was a victim of the deadly virus, and died a few weeks before their planned wedding day.

But love bloomed again, because when Tom Wilkerson returned from serving in the Great War, he began to woo Jewel. They were married by a Justice of the Peace under a big oak tree near Oak Grove, without getting out of the buggy. Sometime after their marriage they bought a farm and built a little house. It was there that their first two children, Rebecca and Iva Nel were born.

Sisters Omie and Elna had gone to live in California, Lynn had joined the Navy, while Virginia and J.D. still lived under the care of Tom and Jewel, as their legal guardians.

Tom had just dug the foundation in preparation of building a shed, when Jewel's father, Dave Adams died. He was only fifty-four years old, but that was considered old enough that young people addressed him with the honorific "Uncle" Dave.

The Wilkersons sold their farm and house to Otho and Sunshine Clark and the family moved to Jewel's homeplace. Tom told Otho that the selling price didn't include the foundation for the shed, so in compensation, Otho and Sunshine wall papered the house the Wilkerson's were moving to. Three more children, Lynn, Hugh Thomas, and Linda Fay were born to the Wilkerson family over the next few years. It was in this house that Tom and Jewel would live their entire lives.

Mama's Mouse Traps

Time went on and the world became engulfed in war. J. D. and Virginia had grown up; J. D. was in the Sea Bees, serving in the Aleutian Islands. Virginia had taken a job in the home of Gussie Adams, the woman who was in charge of the local draft board. Virginia lived there as a nanny for Mrs. Gussie's children. She was dating William Furchess, and they began to talk about getting married, but she felt a commitment to her employer, who was very dependent on her to care for the children. However, they decided they would get married secretly, and just not tell anybody. Another couple, Willie Bee Miller and Vernon Jackson, friends of theirs, decided to go along with them and also get married. They could each serve as witnesses for the other. And so, they eloped. Everything seemed to be fine. A few days later, Mrs. Gussie called Virginia to come into the living room where she sat reading the local newspaper. She showed her a column that reported names of persons who had applied for marriage licenses. Under that was the names of recent marriages. Mr. and Mrs. William Furches and Mr. and Mrs. Vernon Jackson were at the top of both lists. It was a rather long list as several of the boys leaving for combat duty overseas had decided to marry before they left. Virginia was embarrassed and hardly knew what to say. Mrs. Gussie said, "You can just tell William he can come stay here, too."

Lynn Adams was living in Indianapolis, where he met a young lady named Evelyn. He gave her a little ring. They were very fond of each other, but they decided she was too young to get married. She kept the ring.

Later he met and married a beautiful woman, Bernice. She was considered a socialite, and did a lot of volunteer work. She was very involved in beautification projects for the city of Indianapolis, and received a lot of recognition for her achievements.

"If I want Lynn and Bernice to come for a visit, all I have to do is write and tell them we are going to come see them," Mama said, which she took to mean that Bernice didn't want her neighbors to see the country bumpkin relatives. But we decided to go visit them anyway. Aunt Virginia, Harry, Mary Beth, Mama and I boarded the train on the way to Indianapolis. Mama worried I might get motion sickness on the train, as I had that terrible predisposition; I even got sick every day on the school bus. She had tried every remedy she ever heard of to treat this terrible malady. As it turned out, her fear was well founded. Aunt Virginia had brought along some snacks, including some tangerines. She had heard that the white stringy substance under the peel would help with this problem, so I was fed a bodacious amount of that distasteful stuff. It tasted even worse coming up.

We arrived in Indianapolis, and were made to feel welcome. Mama and Aunt Virginia were so happy to see Lynn, their beloved brother. We were thrilled to see our cousins, Jimmy, Nancy, and Sandra. They had lots of board games, and they taught us how to play them. We also decided to pretend to be our favorite cartoon character. Sandra decided to be Tillie, the Toiler, whom I had never heard of. At bedtime, the children were excited because we were going to have pancakes for breakfast the next morning. Consequently, I was excited too; I had never even seen a pancake.

True to promise, the next morning we were served pancakes, topped with butter and maple syrup. I took a bite. Well, I don't know what I expected. Perhaps something like cake? After all it was pan*cakes*. I was so disappointed. And I guess I didn't hesitate to voice my opinion, as I pushed my plate away. They were not near as good as Mama's biscuits.

Again, I had embarrassed Mama. With a very stern face, and through clenched teeth, she told me I must be a good girl and eat my breakfast. But Aunt Bernice got up, came around the table and put her arm around me, and told me I didn't have to eat it. She prepared a bowl of cereal for me, instead.

One day Aunt Bernice took us to a shopping mall. There was beginning to be a real shortage of items for sale due to so many materials normally used in daily living being channeled toward the war effort. For example, women had to forego nylon stockings, as the nylon was needed for parachutes. And many things previously considered as necessities, were now rationed, if available at all. We were in the back of a small store when Mama discovered some mouse traps, which were not currently available at Wiswell. She bought the last four they had. For years she was teased about going all the way to Indianapolis just to buy mouse traps.

Every August all of Mama's siblings and their families came back to our house, which was their homeplace, where they were born and grew up. We loved seeing them. A snapshot shows Papa with Old Red and Old Tobe hitched to the wagon, and every inch of that wagon was covered with my aunts, uncles, and cousins. He would drive us around the farm, a homecoming, of sorts, for them. When we got to one of the hay stacks, the kids jumped off and had fun climbing up and sliding down the haystack. Mama was never present in those rides about the farm, and therefore never seen in the snap shots because she was always in the hot kitchen cooking for the whole clan.

One evening, after supper, the adults were still sitting at the big kitchen table, reminiscing about days gone by when they had lived there as children. We children were outside playing. It was just getting dusk and the lightning bugs were making their appearance. (Our city cousins called them fire flies.) As it grew darker, they came in more abundance until we were surrounded by tiny lights, flashing on and off. Looking into the sky the twinkling stars could be seen through the clear atmosphere. The lightning bugs were giving them a run for the money.

It was a treat, especially for our cousins from out of town, to sleep on pallets on the floor. They were made of pretty hand stitched quilts, and were spread two or three deep, to add softness to the hard floor. We had plenty of pillows, that were stuffed with feathers from our chickens.

"It's almost like camping out," Nancy said.

We laughed and talked way into the night. When I had spent overnights with my school friends, I found their mothers had strict bedtimes, and we children were supposed to go to sleep at a certain time. Mama never made us go to sleep at any particular time; she said when we got sleepy, we would go to sleep. So, tonight when we finally quit giggling, and all was quiet, we could hear the night noises.

"What are those sounds?" Joan asked.

"It's just some tree frogs talking to each other," I explained. "And listen closely and you'll hear the crickets. They're asking 'who ate up all our supper?' and then they all say 'Katy did' plain as day," I said in all earnestness, repeating what my brothers had told me, convincing me it was true. "And sometimes we have birds that are named Will, and if they have been naughty, their mother says, "Whip poor Will.""

The next morning Joan told us that she had trouble sleeping the night before because of the outside noises. She said she was used to hearing ambulance or police car sirens, or maybe fire trucks, but that never kept her awake.

During this annual gathering, Hunter Love, a professional photographer left his studio in town and set up his camera in our front yard. His camera was very large and sat on a stand. A black cloth was spread over the camera, and extended over his head. When he actually shot the picture there was a loud noise, flash of light, and some said they could smell acrid smoke.

The entire family had assembled for the photographic session and finally decided on seating arrangements. Mama had actually vacated the hot humid kitchen long enough to pose with the family. There was one row of chairs, mainly for the women, especially if they had babies to hold. The taller men stood on the back row behind the chairs. The young children sat on the grass in front of the chairs.

Mama treasured the 8 X 10 photographs, but sometimes was quite critical of things she saw in them. While looking at the most recent one she said, "There's poor Gordon. Had to borrow a good shirt from Tom. The sleeves were too long so he rolled them up above his elbows. And he was wearing his white painter's overalls, all he had, I reckon, so for the picture, he just dropped down his galluses and rolled down the bib of the overalls to his waist. And there sits Omie in front of him with that fancy dress on. She went to town and bought herself three crepe dresses. Little Pat is wearing the same outfit as in last year's picture. The short pants are so tight, looks like they're about to cut him in two. Elna and Dennie only have one girl, Joan, but I tell you, she could sure win a beauty contest!"

Nancy and Sandra were near my age, and we always renewed our friendship, when they came for the reunion. The three of us enjoyed my enterprise of creating dolls from Mama's summer squash that had grown quite large. We placed buttons for eyes, attached with pins. We made hair pinned to the dolls' heads, by using corn silks, also from the garden. We used quilt pieces as dresses. Nancy and Sandra had a plethora of dolls, but they enjoyed our squash dolls as much as I did.

Many years later, after Aunt Bernice died, Uncle Lynn reconnected with Evelyn, the girlfriend of his youth. Her husband had died, also. They were married and enjoyed several years together.

She still had the little ring he had given her.

Jewel's New Hat

"Cratic and Lizzie are coming by in the morning on their way to town. Wanted to know if we would like to ride in with them. I told them yes."

"Oh, Tom. I just get so tired of depending on somebody else to drive us to town. Here we are begging a ride and they owe us money. It just sticks in my craw," Jewel said.

"Well, it's too far to walk, and that's our alternative," Tom replied. "We can walk to Wiswell, but I don't reckon Mr. Penney is selling ladies' hats. You said you needed a new Sunday hat. Margie said she would come take care of the young 'uns while we're gone."

It was Spring, and time for Jewel to make her annual purchase of a new seasonal hat. She would never consider attending church without a hat.

When they arrived in town, Cratic said he was going to go with Tom to do some trading at the Hardware Store. Lizzie said she was going to look at some fabric at The National Store. "I always get in the mood for sewing when Spring gets here. I'm going to make myself a new dress."

And Jewel went to her favorite store on the Court Square, Turner's Dry Goods. When she entered the store, she was delighted to see their new hat collection on display. There were black hats, white hats, and a few navy blue hats. What colors the basic hats lacked, were compensated for with the multi-colored flowers or feathers that adorned them. A few even had miniature replicas of fruit—tiny wax lemons or oranges, or even smaller red cherries in a cluster. They were all displayed on mannequin heads on stands. To the left was one of the cloche style hats that had just come in to fashion in recent years. It was almost like a cap that pulled over the head, and most young people now had their hair cut in a short bob, so this type hat covered almost all the wearer's hair; just a little stuck out from under the brim. She laughed to herself, and thought, "If I bought a cloche hat, first thing you know I'd be dancing the Charleston," referring to the dance style that was all the rage in this, the Roaring Twenties.

She stood in front of the large mirror in the hat section, which was placed there for that purpose, as she tried on hats.

She noted that all the hats had price tags on them. She hated to spend $2.98 on a hat. Therefore, she should get one that could be worn year-round. She smiled to herself, "Thinking of price tags, I must remember to remove the tag before I wear it to church," She still felt embarrassed when she recalled wearing her new white sweater to church for the first time. It was a Christmas gift from Elna, her sister, who was teaching school up in Ohio. She thought to herself, "I walked down the center aisle almost to the front of the church, proud of my beautiful white sweater that I was wearing. Something I'd never buy for myself; unbeknownst to me, there was the price tag dangling down in the back. A friend was kind enough to come whisper to me, but all I could do was just tuck the tag out of sight until I could get home. I guess that's just an example of that wise old saying, 'pride goeth before a fall.'"

She had about decided on the black hat with the little black veil, but she wasn't quite sure. The sales clerk had checked with her a few times, making complimentary remarks, as to how becoming a particular hat was. Jewel wanted another opinion, so she decided she would go find Lizzie and ask her to come see what she thought.

She had started over to the National Store, but she had only walked a half-block when a brand-new car pulled up to the curb beside her. She jumped when the driver blew the horn. She looked and there was Tom at the wheel. He reached across the front seat and opened the passenger door.

All he said was simply, "Get in."

As he drove on, he said, "Let's find Cratic and Lizzie and tell them we have our own ride home." They found them at the U-Tote-Em grocery store. They were surprised to see the new car.

"It's a brand new 1925 T-Model Ford," Tom said. "It's got two gears and a self-starter; you don't have to get out and turn the crank."

"Bet you had to pay a pretty penny for it. How much did you have to pay for it?" Cratic asked, skeptically.

"They wanted $265 for it, but I got it down to $255. The salesman said Henry Ford made it as an affordable means of transportation for the common man.

"Some of the young people are calling it a Tin Lizzie," and he looked at his sister and laughed.

Lizzie stuck her head inside the car, "It sure has that new car smell," she observed.

After admiring the new car at some length, commenting on how shiny the black exterior was, Cratic said, "Why you can even see your reflection in it."

Then Lizzie looked at Jewel, and remarked, "I like your new hat. You just decided to wear it home?"

Jewel's hand sprang quickly to the top of her head where she felt the hat. "Oh, I have walked out with that hat on my head," she said in an incredulous tone of voice. "I was just trying hats on, and hadn't bought one yet. I was going to ask you to come look at the one I had in mind. Quick, Tom. Take me back to Turner's. They'll think I was stealing a hat!"

She rushed inside the store, and began profusely apologizing for walking out without paying, "I didn't realize I still had the hat on."

"That's quite okay, Mrs. Wilkerson," the clerk said in a reassuring voice. "We saw you go out with the hat on. We didn't say anything because we knew you'd be back."

Change of Dinner Venue

Harrell and Mavis Broach, and her parents, Obie and Bardney Jones, had nicer homes than some of the Wiswell residents, including us. When it was tobacco cutting time at their adjoining farms, they hesitated to have the workers come tromping onto their nicely finished floors, with their dirty shoes; or sit on their beautifully upholstered dining chairs in their tobacco-gummy overalls. When it was time to cut their tobacco, and therefore their turn to feed the workers, Mrs. Bardney rang up Mama and asked if they could prepare the food and bring it to our house, so the men could come there to eat. Of course, Mama said that would be fine.

Papa pulled our long farm wagon into our back yard beside the path leading to the barn, as Mrs. Bardney had instructed.

The women loaded up their cars with the food and brought it to the site. First, they spread pristine white linen tablecloths over the rough, work-worn wagon. A little breeze whipped the edges of the cloth back onto the top of the make-shift table, so Mrs. Mavis picked up some small rocks that were laying in the pathway, and put them around the edges to keep the tablecloth in place.

Several hens made their appearance from the nearby chicken house, apparently hoping to get cast off scraps. They were making loud clucking noises to be sure their presence was known.

The women transferred all the dishes of food onto the wagon. What a feast! There was scarcely room on the big wagon to hold it all. A veritable smorgasbord! The aroma must have wafted all through the neighborhood!

Mrs. Mavis had made a trip to the ice plant in Murray and purchased a 100-pound block of ice, which was encased in a clean coarse tow sack. The ice was clear as crystal. When she chipped it with the ice pick, she gave each of us kids a shard of ice to suck on. What a treat that was on that hot 90-degree day.

Every Saturday afternoon, the ice man brought ice to our house. We placed a card in our window to let him know what size block of ice we wanted. The card had 25, 50, 75, or 100 respectively on each corner, and the denomination that was on top signified the amount we wanted. He used big tongs to carry the ice and put it in our ice box on the back porch.

But we never went to the ice plant and got ice at any other time. Today the ladies had made big jugs of sweet tea, which was poured over the ice in large glasses, which had to be frequently refilled. The men helped themselves to the buffet; probably the first time they had not been served by the wives. With full plates, they sat on a log that was laying alongside of the pathway.

Though they ate outside, helped themselves to the food, sat on a log to eat, they ate from delicate, china plates, and real silverware supplied by the hostesses.

Randa, Mrs. Mavis' daughter, who was about my age, came with them. I remembered hearing Mama say that when Randa was born, she suffered from colic. Her daddy had come to get some catnip, which grew at the edge of our garden. Mrs. Mavis made catnip tea, which she gave to Randa. According to the story, it cured the colic.

So Randa and I played together. And of course, we ate. It was the first time I had ever seen macaroni and cheese. The little tubes of pasta were fascinating to me. Since we always grew our own food, I wondered what kind of bush or plant the macaroni grew on.

The Runt Pig

Virginia was eight years old, and deemed old enough to help her mother with some of the chores around the house. Her least favorite was churning for butter, and today was butter day. Mary, her mother, had set the churn full of milk, heavy with cream, on the back porch. "I'm putting the churn out here so you can get some fresh air while you work."

Virginia grudgingly grasped the pole handle of the dasher, or plunger, that extended through the lid down into the milk. She hated standing over the churn and jostling the dasher up and down. "Up and down. Up and down. I'm so tired of the same thing, over and over," she said. In some mysterious way that she didn't understand, this action, over a seemingly endless time, made the butter clump up, separating it from the milk

"Mother, I don't think this butter is ever going to come," she complained. This tedious job was made more onerous because she could see her six-year-old brother, J.D., with no assigned chores, playing with their little pig in the yard.

A few weeks earlier, Daisy, the sow, had a litter of pigs, and one of them was much smaller than the others. Daddy called it the runt. As soon as they were born the bigger piglets began nursing voraciously but pushed the tiny pig away; he could not even get to a teat. Daddy mentioned to his wife that since this was Daisy's first litter, she might savage, which is to eat, the tiny pig, so it would be best to separate the runt from the others. So, Daddy told Virginia and J.D. if they would feed it and care for it, they could have it as a pet. They were so excited! They had never even had a puppy. "One more mouth to feed," they were told, when they had asked for a dog.

They were faithful in feeding the pig from a bottle and nipple, until it was big enough to eat from a trough. And then when the bigger pigs tried to push him away, the children made room for him and made sure he got his share. They thought he was so cute; so pink and with such a curly little tail.

"I think we can teach him to do tricks," J.D. said. And now he could be seen tapping the pig's behind with a little branch from the peach tree, and commanding the pig to jump. "Jump, jump!" he cried, but the pig just grunted and seemed only interested in rooting around in the grass.

They named him Roger Pig, and he didn't stay in the pen with the other pigs, but followed them everywhere they went. Their mother warned them to make sure it never came up on the porch, and most certainly not in the house!

Mother checked on the butter churning operation and found it to be complete. She lifted the churn lid and the dasher and set them aside. She ladled the soft semi-solid butter into a bowl, leaving the good fresh butter-milk, which they all liked to drink.

Virginia was fascinated as she watched Mother work the remaining milk out of the butter. She had a little flat wooden paddle that she pressed against the mound of butter, squeezing the milk from the solid, dumping the milk, then turning the bowl to a different angle, and repeating the action, until no more milk could be expressed. Then she put the firm butter into a wooden mold, and when the top was pressed, it left the imprint of a flower in the butter. This procedure of making the pretty design in the butter, along with crafting beautiful handmade quilts, such as Wedding Ring or Little Dutch Boy patterns, was about the only artistic outlets that the hard-working farm wives could enjoy.

Next, she placed the container of butter into a covered wooden bucket attached to a rope, and lowered it into the cistern located behind the back of the house. There, deep in the ground the temperature was several degrees cooler, and kept the dairy products fresh much longer, because in that year of 1919 no one in Wiswell had refrigeration. The cistern was only used for this purpose, for they also had a well for water. When Daddy would draw a bucket of fresh water from the well, and take a drink from the gourd dipper, he would say, "That's so cold it hurts my head!"

After dinner Mother told the children that she and Daddy were going to visit Grandmother, who lived nearby. Grandmother was sick, and might not enjoy the noise of rambunctious children. "So, you all stay here. You can play with your runt, and we'll be home in time for supper." No one gave a thought to the safety of children left alone for short periods, for, at that point in time, there seemed to be no danger.

J.D. had some marbles and he took them around to the front yard where he had drawn a circle, called a hole, in the ground. He dropped all the marbles on the ground, and let them free fall. Then he "flicked" them with his fingers until all of the marbles rolled into the hole. It was really a game for two people, so he took turns; once as himself, and then as an imaginary friend, he would go on the other side of the hole, and assume the identity of the other player. Somehow, he, himself, was always the winner.

Virginia went to her playhouse in the edge of the woods behind the house. As much as she detested working in her mother's kitchen, she loved her playhouse! She had some broken or chipped, cast off dishes, and Mother had even given her an old pan, minus its handle. "I'll never even pretend to churn butter here," she thought.

After a while she decided she would go to the house to see if there was a sausage and biscuit left from dinner. As she came up onto the porch, she was horrified by what she saw. "J.D., come quick," she screamed. There was their beloved pig, head down into the churn, his little hind legs sticking straight up in the air. Apparently, he had smelled the buttermilk, had reared up, placing his front legs on the edge of the churn, and hoisted himself up, and toppled head first into the buttermilk. He had been unable to get himself back upright.

J.D. came running and together they lifted him out. They shook him, and pounded his back. They were frantic! But it was too late. He had drowned in the buttermilk. They were crying so hard they could scarcely see through their tears. Their beloved pet was dead. They knew they had been warned to keep him off the porch, and they had failed to protect him. They had promised to feed and take care of the runt pig. They had disobeyed Daddy, as well as lost their runt.

They got a bucket of water and washed the buttermilk off of the pig, but they couldn't think what to do with it. J.D. was holding the pig by its hind legs, while Virginia was lifting it with the front legs. They carried him along the path towards the chicken house, but he was too heavy to go farther, so they just laid him on the path and went to the house to await their punishment.

When Mother and Daddy came home, all seemed well, so the children didn't voluntarily mention the catastrophe. "Grandmother is feeling much better. She was asking about you. Maybe you can go with us when we go to visit her tomorrow." She wondered why the children did not express any interest in hearing from their beloved grandmother.

"How about some scrambled eggs for supper?" Mother suggested, as she put on her old apron. She would use the lap of her apron as a container for gathering the eggs.

A few minutes later they heard Mother cry out, "Dave, come quick." Back at the house, J.D. and Virginia looked at each other with fear in their eyes. They knew the pig had been discovered.

"Dave, the runt is just laying here in the path, dead! Do you think some wild animal has killed it?" Daddy turned the pig over, and seeing no marks on it, concluded that was not the case. What could have killed the pig? they wondered. With all the attention it had been getting it had been growing and doing well.

"Now we'll have to tell the children," Mother said. "They'll be so broken hearted, for they loved that runt so much." And they continued to ruminate about what could have possibly killed it.

They gently told the children about what they had found on the path to the chicken house, and how sorry they were to have to tell them the sad news of the loss of their pet. The children dutifully cried, which was easy to do, as they were, indeed, heartbroken, but so relieved that they were not being blamed for the loss.

"Did anyone come while we were gone?" Mother asked. "No," they both answered at once. Truthfully.

"Did you hear the pig squealing?" Again, they answered, "No," again truthfully.

"Daddy will bury the runt, while Virginia and I will make supper." When she went to the churn to get buttermilk for supper, she was aghast! "Did you children put dirt in the churn?" Again, they truthfully answered, "No."

"I can't throw out a whole churn full of fresh buttermilk because of a little trash in it. I guess it's my fault for leaving the lid off. Still I can't see how dirt could get in it." The buttermilk would keep for several days, even without lowering it into the cistern. So, she carefully dipped out the dirt.

During supper, Daddy said, "Virginia you did a fine job churning today. I believe this is the best buttermilk in the State of Kentucky!"

The circumstance of the dead pig was shared with neighbors, and several ideas as to the cause of his death were postulated. Mr. Hartsfield said he had been squirrel hunting over in the woods a few days ago and he had thought he had seen a black panther; maybe that had killed the pig. Again, it was pointed out that there were no wounds on the pig, so that was ruled out. Mrs. Rhoda Morris said she had heard of a big hawk being seen in the community; one big enough that it could swoop down and pick up a good-sized animal and carry it off. "Or a child," she added, which cast a pall of fear over everyone who heard this dire possibility. Perhaps that was what happened, and the pig being fairly heavy caused the hawk to drop it, killing it. Still nothing was ever proven. Indeed, the mystery of what had happened to the pig would never be solved in the parents' life time.

From then ever after, when Mother had to leave the children home alone, she would reel off a litany of instructions for them, always ending with the admonition "…and don't put dirt in the churn."

Many years later, my Aunt Virginia Adams Furchess confessed, and told the story of how their little pig met his demise, and how the trash from the pig ended up in the buttermilk.

And until this day when one of our family members is leaving, you might hear him/her jokingly say, "Now while I'm gone, don't put dirt in the churn."

Christmas in Wiswell

We started trying to get Papa to cut a Christmas tree by the first of December. He would succumb to our pleading after a few days. I would always go with him to the back field where he would select a cedar tree growing in the fence row. Papa would chop it down, put it on the slide, hook Old Tobe, our beloved mule, to it and bring it back to the house. He would cut two strips of scrap lumber, making a crisscross, and nail them to the bottom of the trunk to give support and balance the tree, keeping it upright.

"Now we're getting this tree early, and it's a long time till Christmas, so you young 'uns will need to keep it watered, so it won't dry out," he said, as he placed it in a tub of water, in front of the living room window. We were very diligent in carrying out this chore.

The tree might be a little lopsided, caused by growing too close to another tree, but we thought it was beautiful. And it smelled so fragrant!

Getting to decorate it was an act of love. We hung the silver, sparkly icicles, one by one over the branches. The icicles were the same ones we used last year, which had been laboriously removed individually from that tree, looping them over a cardboard tray, and sliding them back into the original box, to await the time they would be called into service the following year. Additionally, we would string some freshly popped popcorn to drape over the branches—if we could keep my brothers from eating it; we pretended this was snow. We took construction paper—red and green—that we had cut in strips, and glued them into little circles, then attached them together to make long chains, to also grace the tree.

Every year on the last day of school before dismissing for the holidays, the teachers always gave each child a small brown paper sack with an apple, an orange, and a peppermint stick, which we called a treat. If I had been asked to define the word 'treat', I would have said "an apple, an orange, and some peppermint candy in a brown paper sack." They were synonymous to me.

When Christmas Eve finally arrived, Papa said we would have to let the fire in the fireplace burn out, so Santa Claus could come down the chimney without getting burned. It was so hard to sleep that night. I thought I heard something on the roof, I was certain it could be reindeer, so I got up, though it was still dark. I begged Mama to light the lamp so I could see if Santa had come. She told me I had just heard the wind, that it was too early, and that I should just go back to bed. That perhaps Santa wouldn't come at all if he knew I wasn't sleeping; that he might consider that as being a naughty girl. That put fear in my heart, for I knew that the homes of naughty children would be passed over; no stop from Santa Claus.

The next time I woke up, it was barely daylight. I ran into the living room, as fast as my five-year-old legs could carry me. I looked over at the fireplace. The fire was out, and there were ashes all over the hearth. There were the unmistakable boot prints easily visible in the ashes. Big boot prints, proof that Santa had come down the chimney, walked through the ashes, and delivered the toys.

Now Mama was no slouch when it came to leaving a midnight snack for Santa. She would not stoop to leaving ordinary cookies, like other children's mothers might do. Along with the glass of milk, she had left a hefty slab of her fresh, made-from-scratch, coconut cake. I had watched her set it near the tree the night before, and now I noted that only a small crumb remained on the saucer beside the empty glass.

Then I saw my stocking, not hanging from the mantle, but merely hanging from the knob on the back of a chair. There was a treat in the stocking: an apple, and an orange, and some peppermint sticks. We knew that when we went to Granddaddy's later that day, he would have a whole stalk of bananas, still on the stalk, something he bought every Christmas. I loved seeing him peel an apple with his pocket knife. The peeling remained intact, hanging in curly loops, all the way to the floor, without breaking. I always held my breath, as I watched, anxious to see if he would be successful in this endeavor, and he always was, every time. I thought he was so talented.

Granddaddy had a heavy mustache, and he had a special cup that had a built-in space for his mustache, keeping it out of his coffee. But sometimes, especially if his coffee was very hot, he would pour some coffee into his saucer, lift it to his mouth and sip it from there. Occasionally, Granny would brown a biscuit until it was crusty, and he would put it in his saucer and pour coffee over it, and eat it with a spoon.

Finally, I saw the big gift Santa had left under the tree for me. There were two tiny little dolls about six inches long. "Twins!" I announced loudly. Oh, how special and meaningful that was to me, as there had recently been several twins born in the Wiswell community.

There were Sylvia and Lynda (I asked- no, not asked- demanded, that they name her after me!)) Taylor, who were always dressed identically.

Then there were Jane and Jean Cooper, Dan and Ann Miller, Charles and Fay McReynolds, Jackie and Joan Butterworth, Gayle and Ann Douglas, and the Witty twins. There were three sets of boy-girl twins; four sets of girl-girl twins; and no boy-boy twins. All seven sets of twins were enrolled at one time at Lynn Grove High School, several in the same class. Briefly, during this time there was one set of triplets: Ludie, Lubie, and Ruby, but they soon moved away. All the discussion about the prevalence of twins in our community made my sudden gift of twin dolls super special.

Also, under the tree were a tiny table and two little chairs for the dolls to sit on. Aunt Virginia had made the doll furniture out of the wooden crate that a five-pound block of American cheese had come in. The furniture was painted bright red. My little dolls didn't come with a whole wardrobe of clothes, as dolls much later would. But I simply got some of Mama's small fabric scraps meant for quilt pieces, wrapped them around my babies, and secured them in place by using a rubber band, or if it was a special dress up occasion, the dress might be held in place with a small ribbon tied in a bow.

The Christmas season was heralded by a huge baking spree at our house. Though we could have a cake any old time - and we frequently did – Christmas brought out the creative, perhaps even excessive, handiwork of Mama, inspired with the dream of producing the perfect cake. And producing them in multiples. She would bake four or five big fancy cakes, some of which would be four layers deep. For this cake-baking marathon, she would buy a large bottle of pure vanilla extract flavoring from the Watkins salesman, who made periodic visits to our house. Mama always bought the vanilla flavoring and Papa always bought the Watkins Horse Liniment. The latter was thought to alleviate some of the pain of aching joints brought on by the hard manual work inherent in the life of a farmer. It was never used on horses at our house.

There would be her famous jam cake made from an old family recipe, which called for her homemade blackberry jam. Next, would be a fresh apple cake with caramel icing. She said there was a knack to getting the caramel icing just the right consistency; a true test to one's cooking genius. She didn't use brown sugar, but rather white granulated sugar, that she browned, or caramelized, in her priceless, irreplaceable all-occasion cast iron skillet.

She also made a butter cake with pineapple in the icing. But the Champion of all Cakes, was her fresh coconut cake. It was noted for being so moist.

Papa's job was to crack the hard outer coconut shell, and then he would use his sharp pocket knife to peel the brown inner coating. The luckiest child would have the privilege of getting to drink the coconut milk. If it was believed to be given to an undeserving child, someone would be sure to say, "But he got to drink the coconut milk last year." We all thought our brother, Hugh, was often the one who was chosen. I was sure he was Mama's favorite! Then, Mama would grate the coconut. It was very easy to also grate one's knuckles!

In that day and age, neighbors frequently dropped in for a visit. They would always be served slices of cake, along with a hot cup of coffee, though they probably had several cakes baked at their houses, also. Of course, we would have an opportunity to taste their culinary offerings when we later paid a visit in their homes. Everyone baked Christmas cakes. But none of their cakes measured up to Mama's.

Perhaps my most memorable Christmas was when I was seven-years-old. When I arose at the crack of dawn, to my amazement, right before my eyes, under the tree was the most beautiful doll I had ever seen! I picked her up, and she looked and felt like a real baby. She was life-size and every feature was life-like. I had longed for a baby sister so long; this was almost like my dream had come true. When I sat her upright, her eyes opened, and it appeared she was looking directly at me. The sunlight caught the blue irises in her eyes, making them sparkle. When I laid her down, she said, "Mama". Clear as a bell. She was wearing a little pink satin dress, with tiny rosettes around the neck. She had pink panties under the dress, with ruffles around the legs. Her white socks and white shoes could be taken off and put back on. I actually learned how to tie my shoes by first learning to tie hers. There was a little card attached to her arm that said, Hello. My name is Baby Sunshine. "Just wait until I tell my neighbor, Mrs. Sunshine, that my baby is named Sunshine, too," I thought.

"Everybody, get up," I yelled. "Come see what Santa brought me." I was not interested in checking out the treat that was in my stocking. Nothing else could interrupt the pure joy I felt with my first real doll. My little twins, relics from last Christmas, though they were my most prized possession only yesterday, were suddenly definitely relegated to second-place in my fickle heart.

I was so sorry that my two older sisters were not there to see my new doll. "Mama, write Rebecca and Iva Nel and tell them what Santa brought me."

My cousin, Pat Foutch, was spending a few weeks with us while his mother, a widow, worked in Nashville. He heeded my cry and came running. Santa had brought him a bright red scooter with a black handle bar. It held no charm for me, as Baby Sunshine commanded my total attention. Eventually, though, I would want to ride on the scooter, and Pat, who would be known forever as my "good looking cousin" was happy to oblige. Unlike my brothers, who would not let me touch anything they got.

Later on, that Christmas Day we took our toys and went to visit my Wilkerson grandparents for Christmas dinner, an annual celebration. It was unseasonably warm for December, so we decided to ride in the wagon. The bigger kids rode on the back, with their legs hanging down. I wanted to ride that way with them, but Mama said I was too little; that I might fall off and get hurt. I had to ride on the spring seat up front, between Mama and Papa. The road was rough, needing grading, so there was a lot of bouncing up and down. I was pouting because I could not ride with the other kids.

Then, as my compensation for not getting to ride with my legs hanging off on the back of the wagon, Papa simply handed me the reins, and said, "You can drive."

I must have done a good job, because Old Red and Old Tobe kept right on going, as if the reins were still in Papa's strong hands. I wondered if the mules didn't know the way to Granddaddy's, and would have gone there even if there were no reins attached.

When I went in their house I bragged, "Look what Santa brought to me!" I was so pleased to be showing off my Baby Sunshine, to my grand-parents, aunts, uncles, and cousins. But I was not willing to let the cousins hold her; look but don't touch was my rule. But everyone was fascinated by such a beautiful, life-like baby doll.

Granny, Aunt Margie, Aunt Lizzie, and Aunt Odie went into the kitchen to check on the food they were preparing. I peeked around the doorway and I could see the top of the cook stove was covered with pots and pans, simmering with delicious aromas emanating from them. I could smell the country ham baking, and I knew that Granny had also sacrificed one of her guinea hens, which was in a pan beside the ham in the oven. Our family didn't like the guinea, as it was all dark meat, even the breast. Since all the space on the stove was taken, she had a cast iron kettle, hanging from a hook over the fireplace; in it was turnip greens with hog's jowl, that had been cooking most of the day. The greens would be tender and the broth was referred to as 'pot likker.' My mouth was watering just imagining the feast that was being put on the table. Though I was a finicky eater, Granny's food always tempted me. No one made corn bread dressing like Granny.

Then, I heard something that would change my life forever. Granny said, to Aunt Odie, "Rebecca sent that doll to Linda Fay. Rebecca and Iva Nel have good jobs in defense plants in Detroit, so it wasn't any problem to buy the doll and mail it to her. When it came, Jewel hid it, and then put it under the Christmas tree before she got up this morning." I heard that, and thought, "She's got her information wrong. Rebecca didn't send it to me. I know Santa came. I saw his boot prints in the ashes on the hearth. He ate all the cake we left him. And he left my doll under the Christmas tree. I'll just run into the kitchen and correct her." And I would have been perfectly satisfied, for after all, Granny was getting old, and quite often was mistaken about what she had heard.

But then I heard Aunt Margie say, "Mother! Linda Fay still believes in Santa Claus. She hasn't learned he's not real yet. If she heard you, it'll spoil things for her."

I was stunned! I was crushed! I was heartbroken! Had I been given the response written by the editor of The New York Sun, to the little girl who asked if Santa was real, it would not have appeased me. I could not be consoled.

Christmas was never quite as merry again.

Plus, I had been good all year—for nothing!

Fourth Monday in March Mule Day

Fourth Monday in March was an important day for farmers in or near Calloway County. This was the day set aside as Mule Day, a time when farmers brought mules in to Murray, (which was the county seat) for sale or trade, while others came to buy. Mules are the product of a horse mare and a male donkey, and they are especially suitable for working in fields as their feet are smaller than those of horses, and well suited to walking between rows of plants without stepping on them. They are noted to be sturdy animals, sure footed, and able to tolerate a heavy work load. While they can be stubborn, most everyone has heard the term "stubborn as a mule", and they may even stand their ground and not move if they are so inclined, however, they are usually quite amenable to the farm work.

By this date, Fourth Monday in March, farmers were about ready to start planting their crops, and needed mules to plow and cultivate their fields. If a mule had died over the winter this would be the time to replace him. Some families might need an extra mule if a son had grown big enough to share in the heavy farm work. Young boys would start plowing before they were big enough or strong enough to even lift the harness up to put it on the mule.

Men might walk in to town, even from relatively long distances, leading their mules, or more likely riding on one and leading the others. Some rode in wagons or even their buggies, leading the mules behind.

There was a sale barn down by the railroad tracks, where the sales were conducted or trades were made. Prospective buyers always scrutinized the animal they were considering buying. They could estimate its age by looking at its teeth, how worn they were, but also to make sure that the mouth had no sores and could tolerate having a bit in its mouth. By manipulating the mule's head during this inspection, and seeing how he reacted, one could get an idea of its temperament.

When a new mule was brought home, everyone came out to meet him and much discussion about what to name him ensued. The mule was welcomed and soon became an integral part of the family. Yes, they would be more like family members than just work animals.

All of our mules' names were preceded by the title "Old", which was meant as a term of endearment, and had nothing to do with their age. There were Old Red and Old Tobe, and the very first mule I could remember, Old Fox.

I can remember my Papa crying openly two times in my life; first, when his father died, and the second time was when Old Fox died. Papa had found him dead in his stall in the barn one morning. He and my brothers dug a grave in the side of a creek and buried him. We all missed gentle, sweet Old Fox, who actually was very old. We didn't know for sure how old he was, but I had heard that some mules might live up to 50 years, if taken good care of. He had no longer been working but we always led him around the barnyard every day for fresh air and exercise, and he got the same feed rations as Old Tobe and Old Red. Our orchard was between our house and the barn, and we often picked up some apples from the ground under the tree and gave them as a treat to our mules.

One day Papa said he was going to Mule Day just to see what was going on, and maybe see some friends.

"Our mules won't ever go to the trade barn on Mule Day, will they?" I asked Papa.

"They certainly won't," he answered. "They'll have a home with us as long as they live." I was happy to hear this promise. Mama said our mules were really just Papa's pets. We knew she loved them, too.

Sometimes at the end of the work day, I would walk to the far field where Papa had been working. He would unhook the mules, leaving the plow to come back to tomorrow.

"I want to ride Old Tobe home this time." I told Papa. "Let me see if I can climb up by myself." I tried to reach his mane with one hand and his bridle with the other, meaning to pull myself up onto his back.

"No, Honey. You're too little to get up there by yourself. Besides, Old Tobe has been working hard today and he's tired. He doesn't need you pulling on his mane or clambering on him trying to pull yourself up. But I reckon he won't mind a little young 'un like you riding. You may be tall but you don't weigh more than a Betsy Bug."

And he hoisted me up on to Old Tobe's back, and then he led both mules toward the barn. I sat tall, and I could not have been prouder if I had been riding a Kentucky Thoroughbred. From this vantage point I could survey our fields; there was a field of wheat so thick and lush that it looked like a huge green blanket. When there was a breeze blowing, it made waves in the wheat, that I imagined looked like waves in the ocean.

Another field was set with tobacco that was already growing. If an occasional tobacco plant didn't survive, Mama would plant a green bean in its place, and then set a tomato plant beside it. As they grew the tomato plant would be trained to climb the bean stalk as a stake. Sometimes when the workers were in the tobacco field, they might take time to pick a ripe tomato and stand there and eat it.

Games We Played

My older sisters, Rebecca and Iva Nel, had lots of friends, and quite often they congregated at our house to play games. The kitchen was our favorite place because if we were playing board games or cards, we could sit around the table. In any case there would be plenty of chairs, the same ones our family sat in to eat our meals. Every meal was eaten, with the whole family together at the kitchen table. The kitchen had a fireplace, so if it was winter time, the fireplace along with the woodburning cook stove would keep us all toasty. There was a particular game called "Guess the animal" that could only be played if there was one person who had never played the game before. Though that person was the target of the practical joke it was all in good fun, and everyone got a good laugh. (It didn't take much to entertain us in those days!)

To play the game, chairs were placed in a circle, and everyone was seated. The game director would go around and whisper in each girl's ear the name of the animal she was to mimic. The first-time player would always be assigned to be a chicken. In turn, each player was to jump up, make the sound characteristic of the animal they were representing, and the group would have to guess the identity. For example, the girl who was to portray a cow would jump up and say, "moo moo", and everyone would guess cow. One would jump up and say "Baa baa", and everyone would guess sheep or lamb.

On this occasion, Ruth was the unsuspecting player. When it was her turn, she jumped up and made clucking sounds like a chicken would make. It was at this point that the game director would quickly place an egg in her chair. Everyone would laugh and say something like, "Oh, look. Ruth laid an egg." But Ruth was too quick, and promptly plopped back down before she had been instructed to look in the chair. "Oh no," everyone yelled. "You've crushed the egg!"

Ruth got up, looked at the cracked egg and said, "I guess that egg got hatched in record time."

It was always fun when some of the neighbors came to our house on Saturday night. We were one of the few families who had a battery-operated radio—there was no electricity in our neighborhood until the end of WWII-- and all of the grownups gathered around to listen. They loved the Grand Ole Opry coming straight to us from the famous Ryman Auditorium in Nashville, Tennessee. There was Grandpa Jones and his banjo.

"Boy, can he pick that banjo," commented Mr. Borden. "They say he's actually a fairly young man. Just made up to look old, like somebody you'd call Grandpa. Then there's Hank Williams, who sings 'The Lovesick Blues' and all the girls are in love with him." Mrs. Cozy, pushed her glasses up on her nose, and asked Mr. Borden where he heard all this stuff about the country stars, and he just said he got around.

All conversation ceased, to listen to Mr. Roy Acuff play the Wabash Cannon Ball and the Orange Blossom Special; he seemed to have an affinity for songs about the railways. "He can make that fiddle sound just like a train," someone commented, and they all agreed.

Everybody got a kick out of a comedian called Rod Brasfield. I heard Mama say, later after everyone had gone home, that his jokes were a little too raunchy for mixed company but everybody had laughed at his funny tales just the same. Minnie Pearl, who always commenced her monologue with, "I'm just so proud to be here," was found to offer material suitable for all ages and all genders, even in the same company.

Soon, all of us children in attendance at these Saturday night soirees would migrate to the outdoors to play. We caught lightening bugs, and they were plentiful, and placed them in Mason jars. We held them up and pretended they were lanterns, as we watched them light up, even more furiously, we thought, because they were contained in the jar. But we always turned them loose, and never caused them any lasting harm.

If the moon was full, we could see to play Tag or perhaps Hide and Seek, until our friends were called in to say Goodnight, and start on their short journey home, usually by walking. One of the adults would have a flashlight, or more likely a coal oil lantern, which totally enclosed the flame, so the wind couldn't blow it out.

Though my cousins, Harry and Mary Beth lived in town, they were frequent visitors on our farm. They came for dinner every Sunday, and often came to spend the day, during the week, too. We played outside and sometimes actually walked two miles to The Wiswell General Store, where we enjoyed a Coke and a Moon Pie, and then we walked the two miles home, though it seemed much longer on the way back.

The boys, Hugh and Harry, played like they were the cowboys they had seen in the Western movies at the Varsity Theater. They got scrap wood and stacked it up, making a respectable-looking fort. We girls were not allowed in. Harry was always talking about his Hideout. It seemed we were constantly running and playing.

And then their mother would yell, "Harry. Mary Beth. Come on. It's time to go home." We played on, as if we hadn't heard her. Again, she would repeat the call, even louder and more fervent. Still we ignored her command. But when she put two fingers to her mouth and made the loudest, shrillest whistle imaginable, all play stopped, and they headed straight to their car, no detours!

I heard Aunt Virginia tell Mama, "Sometimes I think they just want to hear my whistle."

Often, we children played so hard during the daytime that at night I would cry with leg aches. Mama called it growing pains. Said that I was growing tall quicker than my body could keep up, or something like that. She would pull up a chair beside my bed and massage my legs with her warm, but work-callused hands, until I drifted off to sleep. If I opened my eyes just as sleep was overtaking me, I might see her dozing off too, but she continued to rub my legs until the ache had subsided.

Swapping Knives

Farm work usually required six days per week, but sometimes a family might take Saturday afternoon off and go to town. Since these trips were so infrequent people would spend the entire afternoon, to get their money's worth, so to speak. There was always a group of men sitting on the courthouse steps whittling, and discussing the weather, their crops, and, if an election was coming up, which candidate would be best for the job. And of course, they would be bragging about the quality of their pocket knives. After much discussion, an offer to trade knives might be made.

Pete Waldrop recalled the time he was trading pocket knives all day. Sometimes he would have to give a little cash to boot, to get the knife that had took his fancy. Then somebody would sing the praises of his knife and he would trade again.

At the end of the day he discovered that he had ended up with the same knife that he had started with—but he was five-dollars short!

Saturday afternoon in town was a good place to meet one's neighbors. Sometimes the sidewalks were congested by groups of people just standing in clusters, visiting. The young folks in the family might go to the Varsity or Capital Theaters to see the Western that was playing, and it would most likely be a double feature. There were always cartoons and newsreels about the news of the day.

My uncle William Furchess had a jewelry store, specializing in Keepsake diamonds and Bulova watches. Farmers had nothing on him, for he and his wife, Virginia, worked six days each week, and didn't take Saturday afternoon off. In fact, they ended up working for fifty years without ever taking a vacation.

Their children, my cousins, Harry and Mary Beth would frequently go next door to the Holland and Hart Drug Store, where they would buy a Coke. They would sit in a chair at one of the little ice cream parlor tables, and peruse all the comic books taken from the magazine rack, as they sipped their cokes. They especially liked the Archie comics, along with his friends, Jug Head, Betty, and Veronica. The proprietor never said a word to them, but anxiously hovered close by, observing every page turned. The comics were always returned to the shelf in pristine condition.

My First Boyfriend

I was in the fourth grade when I started liking a little boy, and even called him my boyfriend. His name was Glenn Eaker. Yes, the same little boy whose smallpox scab I had knocked off in our scuffle over his deck of cards, with which he played Hearts. All was forgiven for that encounter, even the forced kiss, and he found he could now tolerate little girls, after all. His family had since moved back to Wiswell from Detroit, and he was attending my school, though he was only in the third grade.

That first Christmas after he arrived at my school, Glenn decided to buy me a Christmas gift, since I was now his official girlfriend. Kent Miller held a monopoly on the Lynn Grove mercantile business, yet there was a dearth of selections in his store suitable for a young suitor to purchase to impress a young girl's heart. Furthermore, Glenn's finances were equally meager. After a thorough perusal of the store's entire stock, he purchased and presented the gift to me. A box of Kleenex. I thought this was rather frivolous, and in fact, quite a novelty. At our house we were used to using white handkerchiefs, freshly laundered, slightly starched, and ironed; sometimes they were trimmed in lace, and usually with little flowers pains-takingly embroidered in one corner. Real fancy ones would also have our monogram alongside the flowers.

Of course, the handkerchief might have another function for young women, like "accidently" dropping it, if a good-looking fellow might be strolling by; this done in the hopes he would pick it up, return it to her, as a real gentleman was prone to do, where a conversation might be initiated. A true Southern Belle custom.

One of my best girl friends had an older sister, Hilda, who was in high school. She had a boyfriend who had already graduated and had a good job. When he brought her Christmas present it appeared that he had spared no expense. Hilda showed us her large box of *Evening in Paris* toiletries, trying to look casually indifferent, though I was sure she could scarcely contain her exuberance of being the recipient of such a massive array of fragrancies. She took the lid off the box and let us look at the ornate jars, and pots, and bottles, each ensconced in its own individually molded compartment within the large carton. Even the box was elegant. Every item was made from cobalt blue glass and decorated with silver swirls around the lower half of each bottle. It looked as if shiny cake icing had been driz-zled all over. She even let us touch the silver filigree, but we could not take any item out of the box. The ultimate moment was when Hilda took an atomizer bottle out and sprayed cologne behind her ears. "You're supposed to put the cologne behind your ears," she said, knowingly, "but you put perfume on your wrists, where your pulse beats, as that carries the scent out into the room. Every time your heart beats, it makes the scent spread." I thought Hilda was the most worldly and informed person I had ever met.

Then I started reading aloud the names on the jars, pots, and bot-tles: there was body powder, perfume, cologne, moisturizing lotion, sachet, and a large bottle of toilet water. When I read 'toilet water' her brothers, who had been observing us nearby, began snickering. They made crude remarks, and suggestions as to where the toilet water may have come from.

"Hilda's boyfriend got some water out of his toilet, and put it in that fancy bottle," one boy said.

"Bet I know what that smells like," laughed the other, as he held his nose. Hilda chased them from the room, threatening to hit them over the head with her heavy gift box.

I knew that my boyfriend could never afford anything like this. But he had other good attributes. Sometimes Glenn's class got out for recess a few minutes before my class, and he would go claim a swing on the playground and give it to me when I got there. He would also push me, higher and higher, before he ran off to play with the little boys from his class.

One day another little girl, Dorothy, dared to come request that I let her have my swing. I refused. Why, I practically owned that swing, and was assured it would be saved for me every day. I definitely wouldn't give it to her. To show my authority I jumped up into a standing position; with my feet on the swing seat, I pumped my legs, making the swing seem to almost go to the top of the nearby tree. I could feel the breeze blowing my pig tails back and forth. Dorothy's big sister, Martha, came over, grabbed the swing, bringing it to an abrupt stop, and then proceeded to shove me out on to the ground, and installed Dorothy in my place. Of course, I began crying, while Dorothy and Martha gloated.

Glenn, my hero, came running over, picked me up, and began to console me in the time of my distress. He looked up at Martha, who was in the fifth grade, and much taller than him.

I cried even louder.

He glared at her, and then very bravely, he made a running start, and with both arms out stretched, ran into her, head first; caught off-guard, as she surely never expected to be tackled by a little third-grader, she fell flat on the ground. I could tell she was as mad as an old wet hen. Expediently, before she could get up, the bell rang, signaling the end of recess, and everyone ran back to their classrooms.

I felt such gratitude that Glenn had fought for me, that I decided that I was pretty sure I would marry him when we grew up.

By the time I was in the fifth grade, however, my affection for Glenn had waned. My very own swing had lost its charm, and I joined the Jump Rope Girls Gang; I could see Dorothy sitting languidly in my swing, with no one to push her. She had nothing better to do than to stare at her own feet, as she twisted the swing around, causing it to go in small semi-circles.

There was Glenn playing "Crack-the-Whip", with a bunch of bigger boys. They formed a line by holding hands, and then running in random directions, which tended to sling some of the players off. Glenn was often assigned to be at the tail of the line, where he received the brunt of the impact. Because he was smaller, his position was much more precarious, but he always got up, laughing. He was a tough little boy, perhaps made so by being the survivor of the earlier skirmish with the big fifth-grade girl, who had dared to try to dethrone me, the self-proclaimed owner of the swing.

But I'm sorry I never did play Hearts with Glenn, and I never learned if he was good enough at the game that he could "Shoot the Moon."

My Pet Rabbit…that wasn't

Papa had already burned a plant bed. That was done well before the signs of spring, while there was still a little frost on the ground. He marked off a plot at the edge of a field by placing logs on all four sides. The dirt inside the square was dug up with a shovel and pulverized. Some fire wood was placed over the prepared soil and burned, stirring the dirt around so that all of it was exposed to the burning process. The purpose was to kill the weeds and their seeds, as well as any insects, to stomp out the source of any potential disease. In effect, it would sterilize the soil. The ashes from the burnt wood, mixed well with dirt, was also beneficial to the seedlings, when planted.

Later, when the soil was only slightly warm, the tiny tobacco seeds were sown. Tobacco seed are possibly the smallest seed there are, comparable to those miniscule mustard seed spoken of in a parable in the Bible. A little space around the perimeter, next to the logs, were dedicated for tomato seed and radish seeds to be planted. Finally, the entire bed was covered with canvas, with the edges nailed to the logs to hold it in place.

Mama could hardly wait for me to bring home the little box full of packets of seeds, an annual fund raiser for my school. Each packet cost five cents. She always bought the Rutgers tomato seeds first thing. She was convinced they were far superior, but the Marglobe tomato seed were good too, so she took both. She also bought carrot, squash, Blue Lake green beans, and radish seeds. Then she might decide to be frivolous and buy two packets of flower seed, marigolds and nasturtiums. Almost apologetically she justified her flower seed purchase by pointing out that their blooms were supposed to act as repellents to harmful insects, thereby protecting her garden.

Though, there was still a little chill in the air, the sun shining on the plant bed canvas created a greenhouse atmosphere, and all the seeds germinated quickly and grew at an accelerated rate. This meant that tomato plants would be big enough to be transplanted to the garden early in the season. Radishes grew quickly, so they would be ready to eat soon, pulled straight from the plant bed. They didn't need to be transplanted.

On this day, the sturdy tobacco plants were tall enough to be pushing up against the underside of the canvas so the field must be prepared. Papa was plowing, Old Tobe and Old Red were both hooked to the plow, making the tobacco patch ready for the plant setting. I was following him, walking in the furrow that the plow was making. Barefoot, of course. It had turned out to be a hot day, but the ground, after the top soil had been turned aside, was delightfully cool to my feet. I liked the earthy smell of the soil.

Suddenly a bunny rabbit hopped up just ahead of me. It looked like the plow had pushed him out of the ground. It was a little rabbit, maybe a baby. He was tan colored, and his long ears were sticking straight up. Right away I noticed how white and fluffy his tail was. It was amazing how quickly my mind worked. In that brief instant I thought, "A pet!" And I already had him named. Looking at his tail, I knew it would be Powder Puff.

Then he began to run, and I ran after him. If I could catch him, I was sure that Papa would build a little house for him. Or maybe Mama would even let me keep him in a box in the house. The chase was on. With his ears laid back, he was flying, just out of my reach, as I pursued him across the field.

All of a sudden, he stopped, turned his head so that he was looking straight at me. Yes, inexplicably, he just stopped. Unfortunately, I couldn't. I stumbled and fell on top of him with a major thud. He didn't move. Oh no! I was so sorry. Indeed, I was crushed. Though not as crushed as he was. It was with a heavy heart that I carried the limp, lifeless little bunny, Powder Puff, and placed him back in the furrow from whence he came, covered him with dirt, mingled with my tears.

And so the field was plowed, then disked, and rows marked off. Next, the hills were made for each plant by pulling up a mound of dirt and patting it with the flat side of a hoe. Someone, usually the kids, would carry an arm load of plants, and drop one at each hill. Next, was the really back-breaking job of setting the tobacco. Bending over, a hole was made in the center of the hill using a wooden peg, made especially for that purpose. Each worker had his own peg made to fit his hand, and would be used year after year. The root end of the plant was inserted into the hole, the dirt pulled up around the plant, and tamped in place with the flat side of the peg. Then on to the next hill, where the procedure was repeated, until the entire field, or tobacco patch, as it was called, was planted. Many of the men went from hill to hill, crouched over, without straightening up between.

As the tobacco grew, blooms grew at the top and little supernumerary plants, called suckers, sprouted lower on the plant. These had to be manually removed, called topping and suckering, to prevent them from usurping the nutrients needed for the plant leaves to grow. However, the blooms were left on a few plants, to mature and turn to seed, which would be harvested and saved to use next year.

The most hated job was removing the big fat worms that had tenaciously adhered themselves to the underside of the big broad leaves. To make the job more difficult, the worms were the exact same shade of green as the tobacco leaves that they were greedily munching on. The entire family participated in this chore, checking each individual leaf for this destructive pest. They were removed by hand, and to be sure they had no opportunity to return, they were not just tossed aside, but had to be squashed. If allowed to remain they could devour the plant, rendering the leaves riddled with holes, looking more like Queen Anne's Lace than a tobacco plant. My sisters wore old socks on their hands for this dreaded chore, to at least provide a slight barrier between the worms and themselves.

The ground around the plants had to be cultivated, and free of weeds, accomplished with hoes, and sometimes the rows were laid by, using a harrow. Fertilizing was necessary, and at some point, might be dusted with an insecticide called Paris Green, that contained arsenic. All during the growing season, the weather had a great bearing on the final crop, and too much rain was especially bad, as excessive moisture could cause blue mold.

When mature, each plant was cut with a special tobacco knife. The stalk was split halfway so it could be hung astride a tobacco stick. The tobacco-laden sticks were taken to the barn where they were hung in the rafters, which was a rather risky undertaking. Men had been injured from falls and at least one had died when he fell from the top tier of the barn. Another neighbor, Porter Bradley, fell off a wagon load of firewood on his way to the barn. The fall broke his neck, and he did not survive. Up to this point, the tobacco crop had been a family enterprise, but the cutting was done by a crew of neighbors, who went from farm to farm until everybody's tobacco was cut and housed.

As the name implies, dark fired tobacco required firing, and exceptional skill, perhaps perfected over the years, was necessary for this. A fire was built on the dirt floor of the barn, being sure that just enough fire/smoke to cure the tobacco was generated, but not so much that the barn might catch on fire. Smoke could be seen coming from the eaves, and it was not uncommon to have a stranger traveling by, who was unfamiliar with tobacco firing, to stop and tell us our barn was on fire. Actually, there might be a barn or two lost to fire each season.

At just the right time, and hopefully the right weather for the tobacco to 'come in order' i.e. humid, so the tobacco is pliable for handling, the tobacco is taken down. Stripping, where the leaves are stripped from the stalk and then skillfully arranged into a 'hand' completes the process. (The stalks will be spread over the garden after all produce had been picked. It was deemed to be good fertilizer.) The finished product is placed in big flat baskets, and taken to market, where it will be graded according to quality. Lugs, or seconds will not be worth much. Buyers will bid on the tobacco, and finally the farmers will receive a check a short time before Christmas.

Only someone who has been intimately involved in tobacco farming could understand how a farmer could love the hard work, or take great pride in his accomplishment. Or how the smell of tobacco barn smoke on a crisp Fall morning could be thought of as pleasant.

Stripping tobacco for Christmas Money

As a teen-ager, my brother, Hugh Thomas, was quite an aspiring entrepreneur, looking for ways to earn some spending money, while still attending high school. At that time there were no fast food restaurants that would hire kids to flip burgers, so about the only opportunities he had was to work with local farmers. He devoted weekends, summers when Papa could spare him from our own farm work, and sometimes even after school, to that endeavor.

One employer hired Hugh Thomas and monopolized his time. A minimum wage requirement had not even been thought of at that time, and he paid Hugh Thomas a mere pittance. Despite the fact that Hugh's skills and knowledge of the tasks required of him were approaching that of a grown man, his requests for an increase in pay were refused.

One night as our family was gathered around the supper table, Hugh announced that he really didn't like farm work. "What's more," he said, "though I know I don't want to be a farmer, there's nothing much else for me around here."

Silence fell over the room. Mama stopped eating and laid down her fork. "So, what do you plan on doing?" she asked.

"I'm thinking I want to join the Air Force."

"But you're too young!" She pushed her plate away and took a deep breath. We all knew Hugh was her favorite child, or so I thought, and just the idea of him leaving home was causing her anxiety.

"I've looked into it," he continued. "I'll be 17 next month, and I can enlist if Papa will sign for me. Besides, the war is over, and they say there'll never be another one. That means you won't have to worry, for I'll be safe."

Papa was a proud veteran of WWI.

Hugh was 17 on April 24; on April 25, Papa signed for him to join the Air Force.

We all missed Hugh. He was the comedian of the family, and everyone had fun when he was around. When he came home for a brief furlough after completing basic training, he looked so handsome in his uniform. He was assigned and trained to be a military policeman. Soon he was sent to Greenland, which we heard had been given that name to fool prospective settlers into thinking it was a beautiful country. Ironically, there is little or no vegetation there. We learned it was the world's largest island and belongs to Denmark. Hugh's claim to fame was that he had been selected as a member of the Honor Guard, that escorted King Frederick of Denmark when he made a royal visit to Greenland.

The next summer dragged on, and the weather in Wiswell cooperated, and the farmers had good tobacco crops. This was their main money crop, as their fields of corn and wheat were used mainly to feed the farm livestock or turned into corn meal and flour for family consumption. The work spent in growing tobacco was so time consuming and labor intensive that the average farmer could only manage one small field. However, a few growers were able to raise much larger crops; this was made possible by utilizing hired hands.

When tobacco stripping time came in early December, the call for help was issued by the big farmers. Mama said, "Tom, now that our little crop is ready for market, why don't we hire out and make a little money for Christmas? Of course, the pay won't be much, but enough to see that the kids get something to put under the tree."

The only cash my mother ever earned was from selling eggs, an occasional hen, sometimes a bucket of cream, and now by stripping one of the big farmer's tobacco.

Hugh's former employer asked them to come help, as he had a huge crop. He hired several workers, but he, himself only dropped by occasionally to check on the progress.

Though the weather was extremely cold, and the work took place in an old barn, which was pretty much exposed to the elements, they enjoyed the camaraderie with the neighbors, who had also been hired. Their hands were so cold that they were almost numb, and the nature of the handiwork prohibited the wearing of gloves. But that didn't hinder them from tying up the tobacco leaves into a "hand", which was somewhat of an art form, learned and perfected over the years. This miserable work environment was tolerated by necessity, because heat from a fire to warm them would have dried out the moist, pliable tobacco leaves, rendering it impossible to process them without crumbling. Although this wretched cold damp situation was expected, as one of the men summed it up, "It sure is tough on old bones."

After several days of hard work, the job was completed, and Mama and Papa stopped by the big farmer's house to receive their pay. He met them at the door. Papa said, by way of making conversation, "That was a fine crop you raised, it should bring you top dollar." And when it became apparent that they were not being invited in, he went on to say, "We've come to ask for our pay."

"You know your boy left me and joined the Air Force when I was needing his help. So, the way I look at it, I don't owe you anything." Then he had the audacity to say, in a sarcastic tone, "Merry Christmas," as he shut the door, literally in their faces. There was nothing to be done about it.

Mama recalled that incident many times over the years, always with the same frustration and sense of injustice, as when it first occurred. And she was always very bitter about it. The unfairness of it all.

It stung her soul!

Hog Killing

Hog killing was a big occasion, as the production provided a large portion of our dietary needs. Sometimes we would have five big fat hogs. With curing, canning, and later freezing, we had meat all year long. Of course, we had other kinds of meat too, chicken prepared in so many different ways, and less often we had beef. Occasionally, for variety, my brothers would go to the pond and gig frogs. This was done at night, aided by a flashlight. The light was trained on the frog, which would usually just sit still, not attempting to move away. Sometimes they would use their gig, that stabbed and then clamped down on the unsuspecting frog. Sometimes they would just reach down and grab the frogs with their bare hands. Only the back legs were harvested. I was fascinated by the jerking movement they made, due to involuntary muscle movement as Mama fried them in her cast iron skillet. I interpreted this movement as proof that they were alive and feeling pain. I felt so sorry for them. I would never even taste them.

Some fishermen would come by on Saturday afternoons selling cat fish they had caught in Kentucky Lake. Mama wouldn't buy any, as she was afraid her children might get fish bones stuck in their throats.

At hog killings, like so many of the farm undertakings, the neighbors pitched in and worked together, going from house to house. It was essential that the weather be very cold, "hog killing weather" it was called.

The chores were sharply delineated according to gender. The men shot the hogs, slit the abdomen open to let the blood and to extricate the internal organs. Some people made chittlings from the intestines, but no one in our neighborhood did that. Next the men used a crane to dip the hogs in a vat of scalding water, and then scraped off the hair. They cut off the hams and picnic shoulders, and then cut the rest into manageable pieces, which they took to a table in the smoke house. There the women awaited with their sharpened butcher knives. They carved out the pork chops, tenderloins, slabs of bacon, and ribs. Great chunks of fat were cut into smaller pieces, and placed in a huge cast iron kettle outside, which had a fire burning underneath. Men would use a long handle paddle to stir the fat meat constantly as it cooked. When thoroughly cooked the grease was strained through cheesecloth. This was called rendering the lard, which was then poured into five-gallon cans, and used for everything that required shortening.

The cooked pieces of fat that were left were squeezed with a press made specifically for this purpose, until all the grease was extracted, leaving crisp thin pieces, called cracklin's, something similar to pork rinds These could be stirred into and baked in cornbread; everybody looked forward to having cracklin' bread.

The women cut up the meat that was to be ground into sausage, and Mama made sure that a good amount of lean meat was included.

While Mama took great pride in her talent at making delicious home cooked meals every day—and I can attest to the validity of that—she would look with benevolent pity on any inexperienced cook who required a recipe to follow. She would never condescend to using a recipe or even measuring the ingredients. But she knew exactly what ingredients were needed for her delicious dishes and precisely how much; a pinch of this, or a handful of that, just a sprinkle of something, or a mere smidgeon of something else, always resulting in a perfect outcome.

But when it came to her sausage, the measurements were exact. She weighed the ground pork and to each ten pounds she used a measuring spoon to add the desired amount of salt, red pepper, black pepper, and her own home-grown sage. (And the measuring spoon would not be called into service again until hog killing time next year.) The sausage would be compressed into the sacks made of domestic cloth, prepared earlier.

She raised the sage herself, several large bushes in her well-tended garden. In the Fall she picked sage leaves, spread them on newspapers, and placed them in a cool place to dry. The pungent aroma of sage could be smelled throughout the house. Then she would crumble it and force it through a very fine sieve, resulting in a fine powder, which allowed the herb to diffuse evenly, after a lot of mixing, throughout the sausage. She also used the sage for her delicious chicken and dressing, and afforded the neighbors with sage for all their needs. Everyone felt free to pay a visit to the sage bushes, as desired. Indeed, the bushes were considered community property.

Not much of the pig was wasted. The head and feet were cooked, and the meat was pulled from the bones. From that, Mama made Press Meat, though many people called it Souse Meat, or if you lived up north it was called Head Cheese. It was well seasoned and usually sliced and eaten with crackers. The liver was the only internal organ that we consumed, though sometimes the brains might be stirred in and cooked with scrambled eggs.

Unless they were in school the children accompanied their parents to this work/social gathering. One little boy, Steve, later said that he really enjoyed the play time, but hated when the kids had to pull the hair out of the pigs' ears.

When the sausage was sacked, and the meat cutting table scoured and scrubbed, and everything cleaned up, Mama would go into the house and bake a huge pan of biscuits, and fry some sausage and tenderloin for everyone. A test of her culinary achievement. Favorable comments were always made about the meal, and the sausage was especially complimented. When one family's hog killing was concluded, each of the other families might borrow some of the meat; maybe a liver, or a tenderloin, or a couple of sacks of sausage, which would be paid back when they killed their hogs. Mama always hated trading with one particular family as their sausage was so hot with red pepper that we could hardly eat it. Obviously then I'm sure they thought ours was too mild.

Later, Papa would salt down the hams, shoulders, and sides of bacon in a huge box made for this purpose. This would cure the meat and keep it from spoiling. The meat would stay in the salt for about three weeks. It was important that the temperature remain cold, because if the weather turned warmer, the meat would soak up too much salt, or even worse, might even spoil. After the appointed time the meat was removed from the salt, washed and hung from the rafters in the smoke house. A fire would be started on the concrete floor directly under the meat, using certain kinds of wood, preferably Hickory or Apple wood, and the smoking process was started. Smoking meat was an art handed down from generations and perfected with time. The smoked meat didn't need refrigeration but was allowed to continue hanging in the smoke house. Mama would just take her butcher knife and slice as much as she wanted for that specific time. Country hams were highly regarded and if sold would bring a high price. We seldom sold one of our hams, but around Christmas time every year Papa would take one of the finest to a specific grocer and trade it for a case of canned salmon. Mama made fried salmon patties, which we all loved.

A few years later an antique dealer came by, asking if we had anything for sale. He immediately saw our dinner bell on a pole by the garden gate. It was seldom rung anymore and in fact ivy had grown up, covering the pole. He wanted to buy it but was told it was not for sale. He asked to look in the smoke house. When he saw our table, used to cut meat at hog killing time, he let out a gasp.

"I thought he was going to have a stroke," Mama said. "He said, 'why that's a Duncan Phyfe table' and he even offered to buy it. I know it's in bad shape, being used to cut meat on all these years, even though I always put an oil cloth over it before cutting the meat. I just said, 'no', for if we sold it, we'd just have to buy another one for hog killing."

Wilkerson Farm Life

In our family, everyone arose at the crack of dawn. Papa and the children took care of the animals and did the morning chores, while Mama cooked breakfast. We would always have a hearty breakfast, consisting of eggs, which were cooked to everyone's specifications: scrambled for the kids, two over-easy for Papa, being careful not to break the yolks, and one well done for herself. There would also be sausage patties, or crisp bacon, but more likely country ham. Whatever the fare, there would always be her flaky biscuits, and usually sawmill gravy, except if country ham was the choice of the day, then there would be Red-Eye gravy. This was made by leaving the drippings from frying the ham in the skillet and adding about a cup of black coffee, and bringing it to a simmer. This would be spooned over the biscuits, and maybe over the ham, and sometimes even over the eggs.

There were always many choices of Mama's homemade jams and preserves, made with our own gooseberries, peaches, pears, strawberries, cherries, or wild blackberries. Some other choices were apple butter, pear honey, or Papa's favorite, sorghum molasses, also produced on our farm. A scrumptious breakfast like this was necessary to provide us with the energy necessary for our up-coming hard day's work.

This spring, Papa had purchased a new piece of farm equipment. It was a corn planter, and we were excited to begin its initial run today. From the looks of it, it would be easier than dropping each grain of seed corn by hand, as we had always done in the past. It had two big steel wheels, one on each side, and a seat for the operator in the middle. To the right was the gadget that dispensed the seed.

Papa went to the barn and got our mules, Old Tobe and Old Red, who had just finished their breakfast of corn and hay. He hooked them up to the planter and drove it to the nearby field, which had already been plowed, disked, and had furrows laid by. He poured the seed corn into the dispenser and adjusted the levers that allowed the corn to drop at a predetermined rate. He climbed onto the seat and told the mules to "giddyap".

We watched, mouths agape with incredulity, to see such a modern labor-saving device. "What will they think of next?" wondered Mama.

As Papa went riding merrily down the rows, Mama and my older sisters followed behind him-on foot, I might add-with their hoes, manually covering the seeds with dirt. Later when the corn came up, the plants were too close together to survive, because the ground was too poor to support that many plants. Again, all the family took their hoes and chopped down every-other plant. Much later, research created highly developed fertilizer, that would nourish a full stand of corn, but nothing like that was available then.

In the fall, at corn picking time, there were no modern inventions to make the chore easier, at least not in Wiswell. This work was dreaded, as the corn had to be picked by hand. The corn was dry and the husks (we called them shucks), were dry and rough. Soon after commencing this job, the workers' hands would become raw and sore, and eventually crack, and even bleed. There would be two mules hitched to a wagon, which moved slowly down the field. There was not enough space for the wagon to get between the rows, so by necessity the wagon always ran over the middle row. Two men, one on either side, picked each individual ear of corn in their row and threw it up into the wagon.

Most of the time, it would be a young person who walked behind the wagon, picking up the down row, corn that had been knocked down and run over by the wagon. Occasionally the youngster might be a little too zealous in tossing the corn, and overshoot the wagon, and hit the mules. This could cause the mules to jump or even try to run away, which was not tolerated very well by the men, but was quite amusing to the boys, and anything aside from the mundane job was welcome to them. Fun was where you could find it.

All during the summer, in addition to helping with the crops, the womenfolk preserved the produce from the garden and truck patch. The children were sent, with little one-gallon tin buckets, to pick the wild black berries and dew berries that grew in the fence rows or alongside the road. This was a hateful task, partly because the briars on the berry vines were sharp, and seemed to be ever-present, striking, as if they had a vengeful mind of their own. Despite warily trying to avoid them, they were unavoidable. But also, there was a horror of seeing the dreaded snakes. Every kid could imagine a snake that might chase them, and the prevalence of Water Moccasins, (also called Cotton Mouths) and Copper Heads, gave substance to this fear. Poison oak and mosquitoes were to be avoided, but the worst thing of all was the chiggers.

After getting their buckets full of luscious, sweet berries, the successful pickers returned home to enjoy the praise of those who had found alternate work, allowing them to stay behind. The children felt fortunate to have avoided any snakes, the briar scratches were relieved with a little swipe from a slice of an aloe plant, but the pain inflicted by the chiggers that had taken up abode all over their bodies was not so easily assuaged.

Mama said, "You young 'uns have got more chiggers than Carter had little liver pills!" Chiggers are from the same family as spiders and ticks. They burrow under the skin and can be identified as tiny red dots, which may become swollen. They are accompanied by incessant itching and burning. All kinds of home remedies were tried, such as applying rubbing alcohol, or painting over each infestation with clear nail polish, which was supposed to suffocate them; these were only slightly effective. It seemed the only sure-fire cure was simply 'tincture of time'.

A new crop of gourds had been grown, and some of them would be dried, and fashioned into dippers for drinking water from the oaken bucket. Others would be made into bird houses or hanging flower pots. The gourds were preceded by beautiful blooms hanging from the vines which were trained up the trellis. Mama always told us not to point at any blossoms on plants, such as tomatoes or these gourds. "If you point at them the blooms will fall off and there will be no fruit." It was unclear if she believed this or was simply quoting folk lore, that abounded in our neighborhood.

As the summer came to a close, the crops were all harvested, and the hogs butchered, the meat cured, and the last of the produce canned. Mama would frequently stay up working late at night, while everyone else was in bed.

Later, when we would come home from school, as soon as we got off the bus, we would open a half-gallon jar of peaches to share, and eat them as an afternoon snack. It never entered our minds to think of how difficult it had been for her to pick, peel, and can those peaches. It gave her great delight to see us enjoy the fruits of her labor.

The end of the season work continued as peaches and apples were sliced and dried in the hot sun, and stored for making fried pies; apples and pears from the orchard were kept in a cool place and the delicious smell of the apples permeated the whole house. Peanuts were dug, and popcorn shelled and spread to dry. Cider was squeezed, allowing a couple of gallons to go to vinegar. Pickles of all kinds were processed--sweet pickles, dill pickles, 14-day pickles, bread and butter pickles, beet pickles, peach pickles whole with the stone still in them, and pickled okra. Red pepper was picked, and strung on some twine, and hung on the wall in the kitchen behind the cook stove. Cabbage was chopped and placed in crocks with salt, making Sauer kraut, which the kids called 'crap' to voice their opinion of the much-disliked dish. Onions were pulled from the ground. Hominy was made by soaking large kernels of corn in lye to remove the hull, and then washed well to remove the excess solution.

The potatoes and sweet potatoes, staples of our food supply, were dug and placed upstairs on a big sheet of cardboard and covered with an old quilt to keep them from freezing. Sweet potatoes could be prepared in so many ways: cooked, then mashed, and made into pies much like pumpkin pies, but only better; they made great cobblers, or candied, or even fried. But our favorite was baked in the oven, and we ate them, skin and all, while still warm. The entire family loved them.

Every year on a crisp frosty Fall morning, an itinerant owner/operator of a sorghum mill, Mr. Clarence Adams, came and set up his operation at the edge of our field of ripe sorghum. He was famous as a highly skilled molasses maker, and he wanted to protect his reputation. Consequently, before he would agree to make molasses for anyone, he would have to inspect a sample of their cane, and he would refuse anyone whose crop was not up to his standards. All the neighbors, who passed the scrutiny, brought their sorghum and joined in the process, making their own molasses, too. As payment, Mr. Adams received half of all the molasses he produced. Old Tobe was hooked to the grinder which squeezed the juice from the cane. This required the mule to walk in a continuous circle, around and around the operation. As encouragement in this monotonous task, a feed bucket was tied just a few inches in front of him as an enticement to continue forward, seeking the ever-elusive food.

The juice would be poured into the big metal pan over a fire pit, where it was cooked down to a rich dark thickness, while one of the men continuously stirred the bubbling syrup with a long handled wooden paddle. It would take ten gallons of juice to make one gallon of molasses. As it simmered, a foam would appear, which was skimmed off and placed in another container. Nothing was wasted.

When finished, the thick molasses (which gave rise to the term "slow as molasses") was poured into small buckets, or at our house it would be funneled into brown jugs, sealed with corks, or if we ran out of corks, a stopper made of a corn cob would suffice. The kids enjoyed seeing the procedure, and helped by leading the mule, as he walked the never-ending circle around the fire pit. They also enjoyed taking a sorghum cane, breaking it and chewing it for the juice, then spitting out the pulp.

Papa took corn and wheat to the Lynn Grove mill where it was ground into corn meal and flour, respectively. One field of white corn was grown specifically for the corn meal. As payment for the grinding, the miller got half of the grain. For his half, Papa was given a due bill. At intervals he would pick up the flour and corn meal, usually in 25-pound bags, which was subtracted from his balance, until we had used all that was due us.

Lye soap was made by mixing the lye with bacon grease and last year's left-over lard, in the huge wash kettle outdoors. A fire was built under it and cooked together, resulting in a year's supply of soap, which was used for washing clothes, and for getting tobacco gum from ones' hands.

Corn was stored in the corn crib, and hay bales were hoisted into the hayloft over the barn. The animals would be well fed this winter

When the tobacco was stripped and taken to the loose-leaf floor for sale, this heralded a drastic decrease in work about the farm. Papa could always find a job however. It might be chopping down saplings that threatened to encroach on the fertile farmland; or cutting honeysuckles off from the trees, lest they choke the life out of the trees. Even the sweet delicious fragrance did not save them from Papa's ruthless hand axe.

But it was true that many routine activities had to be done year-round. Such as milk the cow twice each day, feed the animals including the chickens, gather the eggs, prepare the meals and wash the dishes, sew or mend the clothes. And, of course there was always Wash Day; usually Monday was set aside for this activity, and with seven members in the family, it might take the entire day. We had to draw water from the well to fill two big wash tubs and the huge cast iron kettle. Fire was built under the wash kettle and the water was brought to a boil.

In the first tub the clothes were scrubbed on a scrub board using lye soap, then wrung out and placed in the kettle. A long handled wooden paddle was used to jostle the clothes about in the boiling water. After an interval, the paddle was used to lift the hot clothes and deposit them in the second tub of water where they were rinsed well. Tiny little blue balls, called appropriately though not imaginatively, "bluing" was dissolved in the rinse water. We thought this made the white clothes look whiter. Then the clothes were wrung by hand and hung on the clothesline to dry, whether summer or winter. If in winter the clothes might freeze while being attached with clothes pins. We seemed to never have enough clotheslines or pins, so us kids came up with an ingenious space saving idea: we spread the many colored wash cloths on the big lilac bush in the front yard until it was completely covered. We thought it made the bush look like it was in full bloom. That spectacle really embarrassed Mama and she would make her usual commentary when we did something like this: "What will people think?"

While there was still a good deal of work to be done, sometimes Mama would find she had time on her hands. Idle hands are the devil's workshop, she quoted the old proverb, and to prevent any possibility of becoming a laggard and to fill the time, her attention would be turned to "putting in a quilt," as she called it. This gave the women something to do and also provided warm covers at night. On a very cold winter night it felt so good to bury into a soft featherbed, filled with feathers from our own chickens or Granny's geese. And then have all the heavy quilts piled on top of me.

During the winter the living room doubled as a bedroom for our parents, as it, and the kitchen were the only rooms that had fireplaces. When it was time for the children to go to bed in the cold bedrooms, Mama would heat blankets by holding them to the fireplace, to wrap us up, but also would heat a flat iron and wrap it in flannel and place it in our beds at our feet.

In preparation for making the quilt, first, the quilt top would be pieced, either a simple patchwork, or perhaps a fancy pattern, like Lone Star or Butterfly appliques. Most of the fabric would be left over from making dresses or aprons, and seldom was purchased just for quilts.

A wooden frame the size of the quilt was put together. There was a rope attached to each of the four corners, and they hung from hooks in the ceiling. When it was time to stop quilting for the day, the ropes would be wound up, making the quilt go up, almost to the ceiling. Since the quilt would take up most of the room it was necessary to roll it up so that it did not hinder us walking under it. The two long sides of the frame were covered with cloth so that the quilt could be pinned to the frame. The bottom layer or lining was made of unbleached muslin, called domestic. On top of the lining, cotton padding was laid. (Granny Wilkerson raised a little patch of cotton just for this purpose. The cotton was picked and carders, two wooden paddles with short sharp wires on the inner side, were used to pull and stretch the cotton into flat sheets of fiber, suitable for stuffing the quilt.) The quilt top was then placed on top and pinned in place, ready to quilt.

One day a neighbor, Mrs. Smith came to spend the afternoon and found Mama had the quilt down. "I'll help you, if you'll scoot over," she offered. And so they were quilting and discussing the neighborhood news.

"Did you hear about the little ruckus they had with their piano player at another one of the local churches?" she asked. "Her name is Maudine. You may know her, or know of her. It's well known that Maudine arrives early every time the church doors are opened, and parks herself on the piano bench, where she remains the entire service. She is the self-appointed, not officially designated, pianist and fiercely guards that position, as tenuous as it is, against any interloper. They say she is acutely aware that there are some young ladies in the church who are said to be taking piano lessons. From what I've heard, she will probably have a conniption fit if anybody else tries to play that piano."

"I have heard of her," Mama said. "But what was the ruckus?"

"She even stayed on the piano bench when they served the Lord's Supper. That church used real wine and it was served in a large chalice, which was passed from one member to another, each taking a sip. Everyone noticed that when Maudine's turn came, she seemed to take an inordinately large swig.

"The deacon who served the wine told my husband that the chalice was considerably lighter when Maudine handed it back to him.

"But the disturbance I was referring to occurred at a church business meeting. Someone suggested getting rid of the unsanitary wine chalice and replacing it with a set of tiny individual wine cups that sat in a shiny metal serving tray, like some of the larger city churches were said to be using. Maudine got up from her bench and went to where her husband was seated, and whispered in his ear. I guess she knew that women were Biblically forbidden from speaking in church. He arose and declared that he wished to make a counter motion. He stated that he believed the church should continue to use the chalice. As basis for this proposal he quoted what he considered to be a Gospel Truth, 'Everyone knows there was a single chalice in that picture of the Last Supper that's in the Bible. And our Lord said Let this cup, not these cups—plural---pass from me.'

"His motion carried, and Maudine, mission accomplished, returned to her seat at the piano. The person who had introduced the idea of individual serving cups was heard to whisper to his wife, 'She needs to get off her high horse.'"

I heard all this gossip from my place under the quilt, where I spent many hours when it was down—it was like a secret hiding place—as Mama, and maybe some neighbor women, sat in chairs, quilting. Sometimes I would forget where I was and start to stand up and bump the quilt. That caused one of the visiting ladies to prick her finger, and one time even got blood on the almost finished Starburst pattern they were working on.

Papa came to the house one day and said we had new neighbors in Wiswell. They were moving into the house where George and Gilla Windsor had formerly lived. They were Mr. and Mrs. Stanfill, an elderly couple. They had followed their daughter and her husband, Carlisle Cutchins, who was to be a coach at Murray Normal School, which became Murray State Teachers College soon thereafter. Strangely, Mr. Cutchins served the school as a classroom instructor, coach of football, basketball, and baseball, as well as Athletic Director—all at the same time! He had outstanding records. A former football stadium and baseball field were named for him.

Since the Stanfills now lived next house north of us, Mama, my sisters, and I paid them a welcoming visit. We found them to be a friendly couple, but originally from a more southern area. She said she was having to get used to the ways of rural life. She told us that previously she had always "had help" and was now having to learn to do things for herself. Later I heard Mama tell a friend, "I think she's a well-educated woman, but she doesn't seem to have much common sense. Why, she had filled two big wash tubs with water just to wash a pair of Mr. Stanfill's socks!"

In a reciprocal visit one afternoon, Mrs. Stanfill came to our house just as Mama happened to have let down the quilt. She looked at Mama's handiwork and watched her stitch for a while. "I believe I can do that," she said. Mama gave her a needle and thread, along with a thimble, and she pulled up a chair. They worked together, and really enjoyed getting to know each other.

When our visitor left for home Mama inspected her stitching. She was aghast, but all she said was, "I know she means well." But she spent most of the rest of the afternoon laboriously removing the unacceptable stitches. Mama's goal was to make nine stitches per inch, which only an experienced and talented quilting artist could accomplish. She always began and ended her stitching by burying the thread tail between the layers, so that the tiny—but she thought unsightly-- knot would not be showing on the top or back of the quilt.

From then on if any of the kids saw Mrs. Stanfill walking toward the house, they would run inside and yell, "Quick! Quick. Raise up the quilt."

Wiswell Country Store

The Wiswell Country Store, the hub of the community during my childhood was an imposing structure in its heyday. At least it was to my childish eyes. It sat right on the North-West corner of two intersecting highways, now named Wiswell and Crossland Roads. At that time, they were just gravel roads and full of ruts, especially in bad weather. There was not so much as a stop sign at this intersection. It was a matter of who-so-ever-will, as to who had the right of way. Eventually, many years later there would be a four-way stop.

The store was built of clapboard that had weathered by being exposed to the elements for so many years. I always wished someone would paint it. No traveling salesmen or drummers were allowed to attach metal signs, advertising products on the Wiswell Store, unlike the store at Harris Grove. At Harris Grove there were metal signs nailed on the outside of that wooden building: big red signs with the Coca-Cola logo, Gulf gasoline signs, and one advertising Bull Durham smoking tobacco. Some people said these signs might be worth something someday. Of course, we knew no body would have one of those signs. They would just probably rust, like all those car license plates also nailed on the store. Harris Grove Store also doubled as a voting precinct. When Papa went there to vote, he left the kids in the car. When he came out Randy, who had been reading the signs, asked, "Papa, who did you vote for? Did you vote for Bull Durham?"

Inside the Wiswell Store the floor was rough boards, kept oiled, that were always swept clean. The broom, made from local grown broomcorn, was kept by the front door. If a farmer entered with mud on his plough shoes, it was quickly swept up.

Mr. Clarence Edward David Penney had been the proprietor of the store forever. Every time I went into the store, he would give me a penny stick of candy or maybe Dubble Bubble gum, that also had a small comic strip on the wrapper. The comic was treasured, read and re-read, and the bubble gum could last for a long time. It was a momentous occasion when I learned to blow bubbles. In fact, I found that I had a great talent for blowing bubbles with the gum. Bigger and bigger, they were. It was great fun when they exploded back on my face. But not so much fun when Mama had to try to get the gum out of my long hair.

Someone said Mr. Penney treated me special because he was courting my aunt and hoped the special attention paid to me might sweeten her feelings for him. I knew he came to see her, for I had seen them sitting side by side on the settee in the parlor. One day when he left, she showed me the little ring he had given her. It was not a diamond but only her birth stone. "An amethyst," she said. "Same as your birth stone."

"Oh, can I wear it sometimes?" It seemed only fair that I should have my turn, since it was also my birthstone.

He also gave her a new purse. It was shiny black patent leather and it had two straps. I coveted it with all my heart! I wanted her to hurry and look inside the purse. Sure enough! It was full of candy bars. You could buy almost everything at Wiswell General Store.

The store was a good business, and neighbors might congregate there to discuss their crops and the weather that the crops depended upon, as well as to get the latest news. No one would drive all the way to Murray, about seven miles, if they could find what they wanted at Wiswell. But occasionally a trip into town was necessary. Mr. Lee Humphreys, an honest but very frugal man lived close to the store. He owned a 1936 Chevrolet, with a very old battery. Rather than replace the battery, when he got ready to go to town, he would just cross the road to the store and ask somebody to give him a push with their car. After it started, it would run all the way to town. When ready to come home he would flag somebody down, get a push, and drive it all the way home, and park it in his front yard until he needed to make another trip, usually many days hence.

On this day he accosted Mr. Lee Mills, who happened to be at the store, and requested a push to start him on his way to town. Mr. Mills obliged, but he didn't stop pushing him when the car started. Instead he pushed faster and faster. Those watching (and would discuss this event for many days) estimated he was probably going at least 60 miles per hour. Mr. Humphreys was flailing and flapping his arm out the window and yelling "That's enough. It's started" at the top of his lungs. Finally, Mr. Mills pulled back, and allowed the car to continue on under its own power. Mr. Humphreys went to town, and his first stop was to buy a new battery for his car

Mr. Humphreys told the group of men at the store that his daughter's boyfriend had given her an expensive gift for Christmas. "He gave her a new-fangled contraption that plays music. Called a phonograph. I told her 'law, law, you can look at it all you want but I forbid you to play it, because you'd just run the battery down.'"

But Mr. Penney was getting tired of having to be in the store constantly. He always waited on each customer personally, taking each requested item from the shelf and placing it by the cash register; he didn't allow anyone to go behind the counters. "It would be nice to have some peace and quiet," he thought to himself, having no idea as to what was soon going to transpire. So, he advertised the store for lease.

Mr. Jesse "Pete" Henley owned some choice land on Johnny Robertson Road, that would increase in value with time. When he heard that the Wiswell General Store was for lease, he offered to trade his land for the merchandise in the store. The deal was made and he found himself in business. This included the living quarters in back of the store. So, he moved his family to the new combination house and store. His wife, Mrs. Effie, was a sweet, soft-spoken little woman with snow white hair and bright blue eyes, and a face that crinkled when she laughed, which was often. This offset the serious, no-nonsense demeanor of Mr. Pete.

They were raising their great-grandnephew, Melvin who had lived with them since he was three days old, as his mother had died in childbirth the day he was born. He was a friendly youngster, who explored the new neighborhood, and quickly made friends with like-minded kids who were eager to join him in finding outlets for their fun and mischief.

Trade went along as usual for the Henley's, and Mr. Penney was no longer going to the store each day, instructing them on how to run the business, as he had for a while. He was spending more of his time in his big white house nearby. Electricity had come to Wiswell, and he was proud of the fact that his house was the first to be connected. He had a battery radio which he had converted to electric. In the evening he could be seen on his front porch, with the radio on a table by his chair, and his feet propped up on the porch railing, listening to music or his favorite shows. He really liked listening to *The Aldrich Family,* where every show commenced with the mother shouting, "Henry! Henry Aldrich." And in reply, a boy in a changing voice said, "Coming, Mother." He liked *Lum and Abner,* but especially *Fibber McGee and Molly.* He laughed out loud every time Fibber McGee opened his famous closet door and a loud crashing noise meant that everything that had been stashed in there had come tumbling out. But his very favorite show was *The Lone Ranger* and he made sure to never miss hearing it.

Melvin had always been interested in seeing what made things run. Mrs. Effie said he liked to tinker. That he could take clocks apart and put them back together again.

"And they'd keep better time, too, when he worked on them," she boasted.

One evening about dark, when Mr. Penney was elsewhere inside his house, Melvin slipped up to the porch where the radio was left unattended. He attached 100 feet of electrical wire to the radio with a large nail attached to the far end of the wire. Mr. Penney came out on the porch and turned on his radio to hear his programs. From some distance away and well hidden, Melvin would push the nail in the ground, which allowed the radio to play normally. Shortly after, he would pull the nail from the ground and the radio would stop. And he repeated this maneuver several times. He was having great fun seeing Mr. Penney's frustration. He almost laughed out loud when he stopped the radio from playing at the end of *The Lone Ranger* program, and he heard him voice his disappointment at missing the tail end of the show: "I guess I'll never learn who that masked man is," Mr. Penney said in an exasperated tone of voice. But then Melvin got a little too rambunctious and pulled the wire to the radio a little too hard, and inadvertently pulled the radio off the table with a loud crash. He was discovered! Another time, Melvin and his cohorts, tied a string to a catsup bottle and climbed atop Mr. Penney's roof. From there they lowered the catsup bottle down through the chimney, and wiggled it around, which made a noise and dislodged a large cloud of soot. Then the string broke, and the bottle rolled out into the living room. Terrified, Mr. Penney ran out the door, trying to imagine what specter could be invading his space, and spoiling his solitude. Once he was out in the yard, he looked up and saw the culprits on his roof. And other similar incidents occurred way too frequently, and often with the former- proprietor- and- still- owner- of- the -store as the butt of the joke.

When it was time to renew the lease, Mr. Penney refused Mr. Henley's offer. He said, "It would be worthwhile to just close down the store, lock, stock, and barrel, if I have to, just to have a little peace and quiet around here." Eventually he did lease the store to other entrepreneurs, but he made sure that there were no young boys involved.

But Mr. Henley would not be outdone. He bought a couple of acres directly across the road and built a concrete block building. The bottom floor was the new store, and the top floor was where they lived. Consequently, for a while Wiswell had two General Stores. Not so much as a stop sign, but two General Stores!

Moving across the road did not deter Melvin and his accomplices, Larry Parks, Gerald Kimbro, and Jackie Cooper, collectively known as The Wiswell Gang, from their bold and daring feats. Later, one summer, these same boys hitchhiked to Paducah to go swimming in the pool at Nobel Park. It was very easy to catch a ride in those days, and safe for both driver and passenger. Melvin had very blonde hair. Something in the chemicals in the pool reacted with his hair and turned it bright green. Coincidentally, the movie, "The Boy with the Green Hair" had just hit the local theaters. But when they tried to thumb a ride at the end of the day, everyone would just point at his green hair and laugh and ignored the request for a ride, driving on. The boys had a very long walk home.

They were very resourceful; at one time Melvin and Larry hitchhiked to Kokomo, Indiana, to visit a relative. Each boy had ten-dollars in his pocket. They were gone a week, sleeping in hay fields along the way. State troopers attempted to pick them up, but the boys were able to convince them there was no problem and they rode the rest of the way in eighteen-wheelers. When they reached home, they each still had five-dollars.

And so was the boyhood of this youngster. This makes one wonder what happened to this prankster. Did he grow up to lead a life of crime? Was he sent to what all misbehaving kids were threatened with—Reform School?

In a nutshell, this is the rest of his story. Straight out of high school, of his own volition Melvin joined the U.S. Air Force, and using his natural talents quickly was promoted to Personnel Sergeant Major. After completing four years, he returned home and enrolled at Murray State University, receiving a B S Degree in Physics, Chemistry, and Math. Next, he completed the Ph.D. in Physical Chemistry and Physics at Ole Miss. and began his long history as a professor, sometimes Department Chair, at Murray State. In addition to his academic achievements, he was elected Mayor of Murray, and then State Representative for several terms. The first few terms he ran on the Republican ticket, but changed his allegiance to Democrat, to mesh with the then current Governor of the Commonwealth, in order to secure funding for the impressive Engineering and Physics Building, which was subsequently built on the Murray State campus. He served on boards, academic and civic, too many to mention, but included the prestigious Murray State Board of Regents and as President of the Murray Chamber of Commerce. He owned and developed successful real estate holdings. When he finally retired, Dr. Melvin Henley and his wife Rita, traveled extensively, visiting all seven continents.

But he revels in recalling his youthful days spent in Wiswell, accompanied with guffaws, as recollections of his childhood exploits flood his memory.

Wiswell.

Not a bad place for a kid to grow up.

The Wiswell News Column

"Girls. Here it is Tuesday and we've got to get our column written and to the newspaper in time to get it in Friday's paper," Mama said.

Rebecca grabbed her notebook and a pencil, ready to write. She was always ready to write, with her fancy curly letters. (Once when the teacher asked all the girls in Rebecca's class what they wanted to be when they graduated and got jobs, the majority said secretaries or teachers. Some said nurses and a few said housewives. Rebecca was the only one to say she wanted to be a journalist.) In exchange for "Wiswell News" we received a free copy of the weekly newspaper.

"Write that Mr. and Mrs. Otho Clark spent Sunday afternoon after church visiting with Mr. and Mrs. Toy Spann," Mama dictated.

That gave me an idea. "Oh, be sure to say that I spent with Aunt Vick," which made my sisters roar with laughter.

Aunt Vick, an aged widow, was Mama's aunt, and she lived just around the corner from us. Every morning after the cow was milked, I had to take Aunt Vick a quart jar half-filled with fresh milk. I rode my brother's cast-off bicycle, as I never had a bike of my own. When I turned the corner onto her side road, which was hardly more than a dirt lane, it always seemed scary, as the trees on both sides of the road had branches that overlapped on top, hindering the sun from shining through. This made the area look a little dark and dreary. It seemed like a place that snakes would love. So, when I turned onto her road I pedaled as fast as I could to build up speed, then I would pull my feet up to the handle bars, and coast the rest of the way, making certain that no snake on the ground could grab my bare feet.

Aunt Vick was always glad to see me. She was a very vain lady and was always prompt in completing her morning toilette, which consisted of braiding her hair and pinning it up, and "chalking" as she called it, her face. She would only use Elizabeth Arden face powder. She was proud of her son, Bufford, "He sends me breakfast bacon," she bragged, meaning bacon which came pre-sliced from a grocery store. She always emphasized Breakfast bacon, to distinguish it from home produced, cured and smoked in one's own smoke house. Yes, Bufford saw to it that she got the best of everything. Sometimes we were quite amazed how Bufford could even find some of the things he sent her, considering it was war time and many of such things were rationed, if found at all. The answer was made clear after the war ended, and Bufford spent time in prison for participating heavily in the illegal Black Market, buying and selling restricted products.

As soon as Aunt Vick had finished her breakfast, she would dip her snuff, by putting a pinch of the finely ground tobacco between her lower lip and gum. Her snuff came in little round tins with beautiful pictures painted on the lids. One had pretty yellow flowers with the word Buttercups written under it. Another had a picture of a big red rooster. It was obviously a Rhode Island Red. She would sometimes give me the empty tins, and I put them in my play house. She liked to have Rebecca or Iva spend the night with her, and she always gave them a peppermint candy, from her boundless supply, to put in their mouths on their way to bed.

"It will make you awake with a sweet mouth in the morning," she informed them.

She always referred to her late second husband as Mr. Miller, and I was told that was what she called him, even to his face. Apparently, even though they were married for many years, she never felt she knew him well enough to call him by his first name.

Iva Nel reminded us that we were supposed to be writing the newspaper column. "Do we know if we can report on anyone who is sick in our community?" she asked. "I saw in the 'Crossland News' last week that Mr. Carraway had been to the doctor and was told he had high blood." They laughed because the novice writer had just said 'high blood' not 'high blood pressure.'

"We could tell about little Steve Paschall, who ate the moth balls. He is just big enough to get into everything," Iva Nel added. "Actually, his mother, Velma, isn't sure if he really ate any. She found him with several and he had one in his mouth. She rushed him to the clinic. A nurse asked him how many he ate, and he said fourteen. He pronounced it fo-teen. They called all the pharmacists in Murray, and not one knew if moth balls were poisonous, or if they were, what the antidote was. The doctor pumped his stomach just to be sure."

"I don't know of any illnesses, but I think we should announce that our church revival is coming up." Mama said. "We need to be sure to mention that The Parks Quartet will be providing some of the music each night. That will draw a big crowd."

"Yes, and I heard that Rudell Parks will be singing a solo," Iva Nel added. "He has the most beautiful baritone voice. I wonder who will accompany them on the piano."

"Otho Winchester is playing for them," Mama replied.

Iva Nel was taking piano lessons, and loved any kind of music. This love of music may have influenced her when many years later she would name her daughter Melody Carol.

"We could tell about our new cook stove that Papa bought last week." Rebecca suggested. All of us kids were as thrilled over the new wood cook stove as we would have been if we had gotten a new toy. "I don't think any of our neighbors have one like it. I bet no one around here has even seen one like it."

The stove was called Home Comfort, and a traveling salesman had convinced Papa to buy it, and anything that might enhance the baking of biscuits was a sure-fire deal. It seemed to be living up to everything he promised. One of the best things was the reservoir, which was not only a new item to us, but also a new word to me. It was a large glass container that fit on the side of the stove. When filled with water, it would get hot when the stove was in use, and stay warm for a long time. I wanted to take some of the hot water out of the reservoir, but I was not allowed to, for fear I'd get scalded. "You're too little," Rebecca reminded me. It was much bigger than our old stove, cream colored with the words Home Comfort Range in green letters right on the oven door. The oven was much more spacious, too, which was a selling point for Papa. The top surface was so shiny. Black, slick and shiny. "And that jar of polishing cream that came with it is going to keep it that way," declared Mama.

"Put your thinking caps on, girls, and see what other news you can come up with," Mama said. "Otherwise this is going to be a very short column."

"Maybe we could write that Mr. Penny gave Aunt Margie a shiny black purse full of candy bars," I suggested, ever ready to be helpful. "Also, he gave her a ring, but it's not a marrying ring."

"It's not called a marrying ring," Rebecca corrected me. "You're thinking of an engagement ring, or maybe a wedding ring."

"No, we certainly won't put that in the paper," Mama said sharply. "We'll just stop with what we've got."

The Big Old Bull

In the summer following my third birthday, I came to the conclusion that life in the Wilkerson household was just too much of a hardship for me. Especially considering that I had to tolerate my two brothers, Lynn and Hugh Thomas, who were a bit older.

Hugh Thomas, who had been not quite three years old when I was born, had never forgiven me for rooting him out of his very special place in the family—the youngest child, the one who everyone petted and catered to. When they had brought my siblings home that fateful morning, after they had spent the night at Granny's house, Hugh Thomas was astonished to see Mama still in bed. He wondered why she was not up cooking breakfast. She always got up before anyone else. He ran and climbed up onto the bed, planning to snuggle up next to her.

But then someone deterred him in his plan, saying loudly, "Hugh Thomas! Get down off the bed. You might get on the baby." And they lifted him back down onto the floor. He felt tears form in his eyes. He felt so dejected.

Some of the neighbor ladies were there, and everyone was oohing and aahing over what appeared to him to be an ugly wrinkled red thing that was wrapped in a little pink blanket, lying right in the crook of Mama's arm; exactly where he would sometimes lay his head, if he got scared in the night and came crawling in bed with her. Then one of the women lifted Hugh Thomas up so he could see better, pulled the little blanket back and told him to get a good look at his new baby sister.

He was not impressed!

"Her head looks just like a coconut," was his assessment of the pretender to his throne. That description was probably reminiscent of seeing the coconuts prepared when Mama had made her famous Christmas cake a few weeks earlier.

So today, when I decided I could no longer stay here and abide all my tribulations, like constantly being told I was too little to do any of the things I wished to do, and the everlasting teasing by my mean brothers, I had come up with a solution. Yes, the perfect solution. I would run away from home. That would show them!

There must be something better down the road. I was almost certain that Mrs. Nonie Brandon would welcome me into her family. She only had two children. One more wouldn't make that much difference. But if that didn't work out, there were other prospects farther on. There was one family that didn't even have a girl. I knew they'd give anything to have me. Then I remembered they did have two little boys, so that eliminated them from consideration. And so, my intended route was due south. Everyone at my house would certainly be sorry when they realized I was gone—except maybe Hugh Thomas.

It was a beautiful sunny day—finally barefoot weather, something we kids looked forward to each summer. No more shoes to hamper my excursions. I loved to see the sparkling dew on the grass, and feel how damp and cool it was, as it tickled my toes. I did not consider that my feet might not enjoy the trek over the gravel road that lay ahead.

I announced my intentions, as I started across the yard. "And I'm never coming back!" I added. I looked back over my shoulder to be sure I had an appreciative audience witnessing this earth-shattering venture. There were Mama, Rebecca, and Iva Nel, heartbroken, I was sure, standing in the doorway, watching me, while Lynn and Hugh Thomas were outside, urging me onward.

Then I heard Mama remark, rather loudly, as she pointed at the field just across the road from where I stood, "Oh look. There's Stark Erwin's big old bull."

I made a U-turn. Much to the consternation of my brothers, I decided to return to the safety of my home and give my family a second chance. Hugh Thomas was not quite as formidable as the big old bull—just almost.

Vacation Bible School

The annual Vacation Bible School at Sinking Spring Baptist Church was looked forward to with great anticipation. Almost all the children in or near Wiswell would be in attendance, regardless of which denomination their parents were affiliated with. There would be a full week, where Bible stories would be taught by ladies in the church. By the time the week was over the children could quickly name every book in the Bible in chronological order, and perhaps in the form of a rhyme. The older children participated in Bible Drills, competing with each other to see who was quickest to find the Bible verse given by the moderator of the exercise. The winner might go on to competitions at State levels.

Children's religious songs were sung each day, always beginning with, "This little Light of Mine" which would be accompanied with the children holding up a finger to represent a candle, which we imagined could light the whole world. Most songs incorporated animation, often open to interpretation. This allowed for creativity and activity, and was helpful in dissipating some of the ready energy of the participants. Then we would always end with the reassuring verses of "Jesus Loves Me."

On Sunday night after the end of Vacation Bible School everyone came to enjoy seeing the children present their closing program. The children came early to run through the rehearsal once more. At the end of rehearsal, some of the kids darted out the side door to play for a few minutes before performing. Some of them picked up some little green apples from under the tree growing in the yard next to the cistern and were eating them. Miss Zera Parks came out and shooed the children back inside. "Be careful you don't get your pretty clothes dirty with those juicy apples," she chided them, as she got them lined up to go back on the stage when it was time to start.

The pulpit served as the stage and behind the stage, hanging on the wall was a burgundy colored velvet banner, with the words "GOD IS LOVE." It had been there all my life; nearly six years. Nearby was a scoreboard that showed the number of members who had attended the morning service, as well as the amount of tithes and offerings collected. In the back of the sanctuary was the little nursery with two little cribs. And in another corner hung the rope to be pulled to ring the bell on top of the building that called worshippers to church.

If we got to church early enough for Sunday morning services, I could see Mr. John Warren, the church sexton, hold up little Larry Wilson, to let him pull the heavy rope and ring the bell. I wanted to ring the bell but I was told I was too little.

As the audience filed in and were seated, Miss Zera marched the children onto the stage. Each child who attended was given a part in the program, though some were just toddlers. One of the youngest children was Jerry Parks, and his memory verse was the shortest verse in the Bible, in keeping with his age. That was John 11: 35 *Jesus wept.* But when he said his verse it came out something like "gee gee whup."

A pretty little girl in a yellow dotted swiss dress stepped forward, pulled her dress up daintily, and swaying back and forth, said, "My grandmother made my dress last night." When the laughter died down, she continued with "She didn't get it finished, so she has a lot of pins holding it together."

One little tyke, whose mother stood on the floor at the edge of the stage, holding his hand, to help him stay in line, managed to wriggle from her grasp and made a belly flop out onto the floor. He wasn't hurt, and was willing to return to his place on stage.

All the memory verses were quoted by the children with only a little prompting at strategic points. Just as the closing song was coming up, suddenly a little boy on the back row began to throw up. Then a little girl on the front row was sick. From the looks of things, it was apparent that the little green apples were the culprits. Mothers made their ways to the stage to claim their children, just as one child was heard to loudly say, "Hurry. I need to go to the toilet."

Everyone agreed that the closing program culminated a very successful Vacation Bible School.

The Dough Boy

He said penmanship was considered an important subject in school when he was a boy. And he had a beautiful cursive handwriting, very clear and easy to read, yet fancy, bordering on calligraphy. His father, Hunter Wilkerson, sent him to school, though he might have kept him home after his completing the very early grades, when he got big enough to help on the farm. Many farmers did that. He remembers that his father, a strict disciplinarian, to emphasize the family sacrifice that his class attendance cost them in work hours, told him, "Tom, you remember you're going to school to learn. And I'd better not hear of you wasting your time playing!"

But what was a child to do at recess? He played like all the children did. One day in a game of Tug of War, his hand slipped off the rope and was mashed against some rocks. He knew his finger was broken, but he feared he would not be allowed to attend school if his Dad found out he had been participating in a game. He never told anyone at school or at home. He worked in the fields every afternoon after school and on week-ends, being careful to hide his bruised and swollen finger from view.

He said on his very first day of school, his Dad bought two no. 2 yellow pencils. He gave him one; then he broke the other one into two pieces, and gave one-half each to the two girls, Lizzie and Margie. So was the special advantage of being the oldest male child.

In his later years, I would occasionally find his signature written on scrap paper, on junk mail, or even on the margins of the newspaper. It was like he was practicing his penmanship. Now, many years later I still have his little note pad and New Testament that he carried all through the war, as well as a cigar box—all of which have his handwritten signature on them. Sometimes he would write Thomas S. Wilkerson, or Tom Wilkerson, or T.S. Wilkerson, or even his full legal name: Thomas Samuel Wilkerson. Having signed his name so many different ways became a brief problem when Social Security and Medicare came into being, as his full signature was required on all the legal documents. As a kid growing up, his friends all had nicknames, and he was called Tom Cat. But to his mother he was always Tommy. Many years later, when I came along, I would call him Papa.

As a young man, he was quickly following in his father's footsteps in becoming a farmer, and perhaps he might have spent his life without venturing too far from Wiswell, but in 1917 he was drafted into the United States Army. Calloway County had a quota of 136 men—two groups of 50, then the balance to follow. The balance was changing as occasionally previously selected men failed their physicals or received exemptions. Albert Camp, whose name was listed in the current group had a "hunting accident" and shot off two fingers; it happened the same day he was to report to the draft board. He was sent to the hospital but was told to report with the second group about a week later. The local newspaper, The Ledger and Times, had published the names of these men, and in an accompanying article had invited the public to come to the train station to bid these soon-to-be-soldiers a fond farewell. The invitees were exhorted to come with a cheerful, encouraging attitude, and leave your tears at home.

The inductees were transported by train first, to Camp Zachery Taylor for examinations, which would determine if they were suitable for military duty. Some were deferred if in a strategic occupation, such as farming. Why Tom was not deferred on that account is not known. He was sent to Camp Shelby, Mississippi for basic training. (Almost exactly 65 years later, his daughter, LT. COL Linda Fay Clark, served in the United States Army at the same installation for a brief training session.)

While he was at Camp Shelby his father decided to check on him. He walked almost all the way from Wiswell to the camp, which was at the southern boundary of Hattiesburg, Mississippi. The security at the camp was apparently very lax, as he was allowed to stay several days, eating with the soldiers in their mess hall, and even sleeping on a cot in the barracks.

War had already been raging in Europe for three years, but President Woodrow Wilson was determined that the United States would remain neutral, and not enter the fighting. However, when the Germans began sinking civilian ships, including luxury liners, with many Americans on board, on April 6, 1917, he asked Congress to declare war on Germany and her allies.

And so, PVT Wilkerson was sent to the European battle front by troop ship, where he fought in France and Germany.

This was the first time that American soldiers were sent to protect foreign soil!

He never spoke much about combat, or the horrors he had witnessed, or the trenches he had crawled in, but he never ceased being amazed that he had seen so much of the world. I heard him tell anyone who would listen, "I washed my face and hands in the Rhine River." And this was also true of the Seine. Places he had just read about in books as a school boy, never dreaming he would have that experience. He was a member of the

Army Engineers, involved in the strategic operation of building bridges and roads. He said their slogan was, "Join the Engineers and see the world—by the shovel full!"

It came to be known as The Great War. It was touted as "The war to end all wars." Therefore, there seemed to be no need to designate it as World War I, as there was never supposed to be another world war to distinguish it from.

PVT Wilkerson was promoted to PFC Wilkerson while on the battlefield. Always underestimating his valuable contributions, he laughed and said he suspected his chance of promotion had been enhanced by the fact that he loaned his Captain two dollars until payday.

General Black Jack Pershing was the Commander of the American Expeditionary Forces, and he surprised the enemy by how quickly he had the American soldiers on the battle front. In the beginning Pershing already had 127,500 men; by the end of the war over 4 million had served in the United States Army, with an additional 800,000 in other branches of the military. The American soldiers were nicknamed "Doughboys" by some, though no one seems to agree why. Some said it was because the large brass buttons on their uniform looked like dinner rolls. Others said it was a holdover from the military operations on the Mexican border where the infantry marched in white adobe dust, which covered them in a white film; thence they were called "dobies" and eventually changed to Doughboys

Another name heard was the "Yanks", which the British especially used in referring to the most welcome addition of the Americans. When the British soldiers heard they were to be joined by American Forces they were greatly encouraged. The quick response lifted the British soldiers' morale, leading to enhanced success on the battle front.

George M. Cohan wrote a very popular song, titled "Over There." The soldiers sang it themselves sometimes, as they marched in cadence to the tune. In part it was:

Over There

Over there, over there

Send the word, send the word over there

That the yanks are coming

The yanks are coming

The drums rum-tumming

Everywhere

So prepare, say a prayer

Send the word, send the word to beware

We'll be over, we're coming over

And we won't be back till it's over

Over there

His military service was a source of great pride to Papa, and had bearing on his life in many ways. When he came home from the war, and asked Jewel Adams to marry him, they had to decide on a date. They decided they would marry the following October. But then to decide a day.

"Let's make it October 13, the anniversary of my induction into the Army," he said. Mama, being just a little superstitious said, "The 13th? Just as long as it's not Friday."

In World War I, the average enlisted soldier during his first year received approximately $30 per month, which would be equal to $558.12 today. For this amount he was expected to fight in hand-to-hand combat with the Germans and their Allied powers.

In 1922 the Bonus Act that was proposed as supplemental pay for World War I Veterans was vetoed by President Harding. Then President Coolidge made his famous statement "patriotism…bought and paid for is not patriotism" and he also vetoed the bill. Papa told the story of how the American Legion continued to fight for the Bonus Act, but objected to the term 'bonus' because bonus has come to mean "full payment *plus*" and there has not been full payment...so there cannot be any payment *plus*. Three Presidents came and left office before the Bonus Act was ratified. Even President Franklin Delano Roosevelt vetoed the bill, but Congress overrode him, and the payments were made to the veterans in 1936, while the country was still in the throes of the Great Depression.

The Bonus Act paid the World War I Veterans $1 per day for every day spent in service in the United States, and $1.25 per day for every day spent overseas.

Papa's payment was received and was responsible for his being able to pay his taxes during the Great Depression, as he had lost all of his money when the banks closed. He also loaned a neighbor enough money to pay his taxes. Two farms were saved from foreclosure. There are some discrepancies as to exactly how long the depression lasted. It really didn't matter how long the records show, because for anyone who lived through it, it lasted forever.

Mama said she made a little bag from the unbleached domestic cloth, left from making quilt linings. She kept their money in the bag, pinned to her underclothing. Even working in the field, she was acutely aware of where their small savings were at all times.

Papa had a knack for storytelling, and he loved telling his stories to children. His first grandchild was a boy named James Allen. James lived with his family in Michigan, but he spent a few weeks with us on the farm every summer. The biggest treat in the world for James was when Papa Tom would load him up in his old truck and go to the Wiswell General Store for a Coca-Cola and a candy bar. To get to the store they had to go over the Wiswell bridge. For several years James believed that the Wiswell Bridge belonged to him, because Papa Tom had given it to him.

Papa was blessed with a great, though subtle, sense of humor. One day in his later years, I gave him a pill that his doctor had just prescribed for him. He seldom took any medication. An infrequent little toddy at bed-time cured most things right away. He took the new pill in his hand and scrutinized it, noticing it was scored. "Why has it got this crease in it?"

"That's because some patients would only need one-half tablet, so it's scored to make it easier to break in two." I explained.

"Oh," and without even smiling, "I thought it was in case it got stuck in my throat you could take a screwdriver to it."

I told one of my nurse colleagues about his assessment of his pill, and we had a good laugh. She said, "My dad has a great sense of humor, too. He tells 100 jokes a day. Unfortunately, it's the same one!"

The Wiswell Fly Boys
of World War II

When the United States military draft was initiated in 1940, most of those called up were very young single men. Actually, most were teenagers. But as war was declared, and time went on, the pool of single men was almost depleted. Consequently, more and more married men, men with children, and even older men were called. But anyone engaged in full time farming was deferred.

MAJ. Jimmy Stewart—yes, the movie star—had been drafted as an enlisted man, early in the war. But he was rejected because he was so underweight for his height. He felt a strong sense of duty to his country, so he was determined to gain weight to meet the requirements. He was successful, so he volunteered for the Army Air Corp, where he trained as a pilot.

James Warren Erwin, who lived in Wiswell, was also a pilot with the Army Air Corp. He accompanied MAJ. Stewart in his B-24 on at least one mission, not in combat, but they dropped supplies to the American troops behind German lines.

When James Warren was drafted, he was sent for training somewhere in Virginia. He and his girlfriend, Polly, who was waiting back home, began to regret not getting married before he had left. He wrote her and told her to come to the town near where he was stationed and they would get married. Eighteen-year-old Polly rode a bus alone, which was considered quite daring, to travel, unchaperoned. He met her, and they were married. Her mother had hoped they could have had a fancy wedding, but it was with her blessing that they had followed their hearts. She decided that at least they must have a traditional wedding cake. So, she baked a cake, boxed it up and mailed it to them. They were able to live together until he was sent overseas. She then returned to her parents' home to await his return.

James Warren's first military plane was a B-24 Bomber, and he named it "Polly's Pet" after his wife. The name and a picture representing Polly were emblazoned on the side of the air craft. He said he never named any of the subsequent planes that he flew because they were usually destroyed before he could do so.

On one of his missions his plane was hit by shrapnel, making a loud noise and jarring it about, but not heavily damaged. His co-pilot, who evidently thought they were about to crash, exited the plane. James Warren grabbed for him, to restrain him, but he was out of reach. The co-pilot parachuted to the ground and was taken prisoner by the Germans. He survived the imprisonment and was freed at the end of the war, when he returned to the United States.

Soldiers' letters were censored by military personnel, to protect any sensitive information from being leaked to the enemy. Censorship was obliteration of anything that might be construed as information helpful to the enemy, such as location of the troops or any planned military activities for the future, or anything that could be linked to espionage or intelligence gathering. Sometimes the forbidden messages might be blacked out or even actually cut from the paper. There was no charge to the soldiers for postage; they simply wrote "free" where the stamp would usually be attached.

James Warren and Polly developed a code that allowed some forbidden information to appear as innocent and escape the censor's tool. He had attended high school at Lynn Grove, and it seemed all the kids there had nicknames. "Jaybird" happened to be his. So, Polly might write, "Do you know where old Jaybird is?" And he could give information so that she could get a general idea of his whereabouts.

He flew a total of 33 missions, with the 13th mission occurring on D-Day. He returned home as a hero. Polly made glass cased shadow boxes to display all of his medals and citations.

Brooks Underwood, another boy from Wiswell, was a tail gunner on a B-52 during World War II. His role on the fighter bomber was to defend against enemy planes that were attacking from the rear. The tail gunner had to sit in a tight and cramped compartment where he operated the two automatic weapons, firing upon any enemy fighters approaching from the rear. The tail gunner position was essential to protect his plane and its crew, because until this position was created, the rear of the plane was very vulnerable to enemy attack.

His mother received a letter from the United States Air Corp Official commending her son for his brave service, completing more than 30 missions over Germany. Coincidentally Cpl. Underwood also flew a sortie with MAJ. Jimmy Stewart. I'm sure Stewart was impressed with these fly boys from Wiswell. Brooks made it home after the war, married Euple Erwin, and they had two children, Sharon and Johnny. But Brooks died at the very young age of 43 from a massive heart attack.

Another bombardier from Wiswell was Hampton Erwin, who flew missions in the Pacific war zone. He was one of ten in his flight training group. One member was killed during practice exercise. Another was shot down and killed on his very first mission over Japan. The remaining eight survived.

COL. Erwin's plane was shot down and he landed in shark infested waters. Luckily, he was soon rescued by allies. He had an illustrious and long career, and retired with a chest full of medals and certificates and awards.

We had just heard some terrible news. Our neighbor, Mrs. Irene Hopper, had received word that her brother, James Pate had been killed. Mama took me with her as she went to offer her condolences. When we arrived, I was disturbed to see Mrs. Hopper crying uncontrollably. Her eyes were puffy and her face was tear stained. She was walking the floor, and could not be consoled.

"I was so much older than him, I felt more like he was my child than my brother. I practically raised him," she explained. "I can't believe he is gone. I keep hoping I'll wake up from this terrible nightmare."

James Pate was a member of a crew that flew gliders behind Germany lines. He was killed on D-Day in Normandy, France. A memorial service was held for him at Sinking Spring Baptist Church in Wiswell.

The D-Day victory was considered to be the turning point of the war.

From Normandy to the Battle of the Bulge*

Roy Hoffman Swann, a soldier from Murray, was inducted into the army four days after his 31st birthday. The draft pool of very young men was nearly depleted, and so by necessity older men were also being called to serve. He was assigned to the 379th Infantry, 3rd Battalion of the 95th Division, which became a part of General Patton's Third Army. Later, his discharge would show that he had served three years and four months in the strategic position of Intelligence NCO. And it further stated that he assisted in the interpretation and distribution of information of enemy and counter-intelligence and the safeguarding of Military information; maintained the situation, strength, and probable intentions, and interrogated the enemy prisoners....

He was not in the first wave of service men who stormed the Beach at Normandy. His group had come in as reinforcement for the soldiers who were in the initial landing. He knew that James Pate, a soldier from home, had been with the first group who had landed on the beach. When things had quieted down somewhat, he asked a Lieutenant with the first group if Cpl. James Pate was there. The Lieutenant, pointing to the few haggard, exhausted, battle-weary men sitting or lying beside the road, said, "You can look over there and see. That's all that's left of them." James Pate was not among them.

Sgt. Swann's battalion pressed on, in the face of stiff opposition from the Germans. He participated in the famous Battle of the Bulge, that lasted from December 16, 1944 until January 25, 1945. Not only did they have to face the desperate German army, but also the bitterest, record-breaking cold winter. During this time the snow fall was extremely heavy. In the daytime they wore white capes with hoods as camouflage. In a letter to his mother, he wrote, "The people moved like ghosts over the white snow."

The letters he wrote were sent by airmail in envelopes that had patriotic red, white, and blue stripes along the edges. One, postmarked February 13, 1945, sent to his then girlfriend, Mary Lou Outland, had the handwritten signature of the censor, who had dutifully read the outgoing letter. Beside the signature was a code number and it was stamped Passed.

A glossy pictorial journal titled "The 95th Infantry Division's Road to Victory Through the ETO (European Theater of Operation)" containing photographs taken by the U.S. Signal Corps was given to each of the soldiers who participated in these battles and is among the memorabilia left by Mr. Swann. In it, there is a full-page photograph of a huge banner, stretching across a major highway at the border of Germany. On this banner, in gigantic letters, victory was being proclaimed with the following: YOU ARE NOW ENTERING GERMANY THRU COURTESEY OF 95th INFANTRY DIVISION. Crossing into Germany under this sign were soldiers who were walking through a deep slosh of snow and miring mud, made worse by the pounding of thousands of boots.

In the journal there was also a schematic drawing of a map with a line tracing the route where these invasion forces started in England, going across the English Channel and onto Omaha Beach; then on into France through Paris to Belgium, from where Sgt. Swann wrote that he was "in and out of Germany several times." Eventually they were in combat in Holland.

Hoffman Swann also related another interesting incident that occurred while he served overseas. He discovered that a young man he knew from back home was in a nearby military hospital in France. His name was Robert Hendon, and he had just had a battle injury so severe that an arm had to be amputated. Hoffman wanted to write and send word to the family about him, as he knew it might take weeks before they were informed through the slow-moving routine channels. Yet, he knew that if he wrote the information outright, the censor would just delete it. He remembered that there was a well-known man who still lived in his home town named Rubin Falwell, who only had one arm. So, he wrote a letter to his mother that said, "I saw Robert Hendon today. He is fine but now he looks just like Rubin Falwell." He knew his mother would pass the word to Robert's family.

*Information presented above is based on personal conversations with Mr. Swann, letters he wrote from the battlefields to family members, and his Honorable Discharge, as well as records from the 95th Division.

It was reported by several parents in my neighborhood that they had received information about the wounding or death of their sons from letters written to them by their sons' buddies, well in advance of the notification by the War Department. There were also incidents when the War Department accidently issued erroneous reports to the families. Case in point was when a local family received word that their son was killed in action. They were already in the process of planning a memorial service when they received the joyous news that he was alive. In fact, this message came in the form of a letter from their son, himself. He had been taken prisoner of war by the Germans, and his letter to his parents had been expedited by the Red Cross. Conversely, it was said that some families had been reassured when they received word that their son had been wounded but was alive, only to hear soon afterward that in fact he had been killed in action.

There were two soldiers who were very special to me. First, Fred Cooper, who was engaged to my sister, Rebecca. They faithfully wrote letters, and she awaited his return, while she worked in a defense plant in Detroit. Rosie the Riveter could have been patterned after her. They were married when he returned home, and they had one daughter, Marilyn, who was a beautiful child, in fact would have been perfect if she only had curly hair.

The second was Albert Hughes, who was engaged to my other sister, Iva Nel. Though they didn't end up getting married, we continued to follow his service. And I was broken hearted to learn that he had been killed. I attended his funeral at Sinking Spring Baptist Church. Hearing taps played on a bugle by a young man in dress uniform brought tears to my eyes. To see the folded American flag presented to his mother made me feel so patriotic. The military services were hugely impressive and included a twenty-one-gun salute, which was very grand, but terribly frightening to hear. He also had three brothers in the Armed Service at the same time. They all returned home safely.

Kerby Jennings was the editor of The Murray Democrat, a weekly newspaper that served Wiswell and surrounding areas in Calloway County. He was a very civic minded and patriotic citizen. He knew that letters were so important to the soldiers, who were often teenagers, away from home for the first time. Likewise, letters from the soldiers to family and friends were longed for and could be reassuring. Knowing that the soldiers might not be able to write multiple individual letters to everyone at home, Mr.

Jennings came up with an original idea. He invited the service members to write letters directly to the newspaper, and he would publish them, alongside their pictures, which he had on file. They looked so brave—and so serious, in their uniforms.

The column was titled "Hard Tack and Sea Soup." Each week when the paper came out, everyone scrambled to read the letters from the soldier boys. And the soldiers received many letters in response. Apparently, Mr. Jennings sent his newspaper directly to the soldiers, as Hoffman Swann mentioned in one of his letters, "I read about that in the Calloway paper."

There was one young man, Tom, who wrote frequently, who always spoke of looking forward to winning the war and coming home. He ended every letter by saying, "This is Tom. Let's give them the bomb. I'll be coming home before you know it." We were particularly saddened when Papa read his latest letter, turned the page and saw Tom's death notice in the same issue.

It was very common for families to have several sons on active duty at the same time. Unfortunately, it was not unusual to have multiple casualties of war in the same family, also. Framed gold stars, placed in front windows were way too common. People said when they heard someone approaching their door step, they were afraid to see who it was. They were afraid it might be a messenger bringing the dreaded telegram informing them of the death of their loved one. Wiswell gave many of its young men to service, and some paid the supreme sacrifice.

A Troop Train Romance

Riley Gunter was a man who idolized Theodore Roosevelt, former President of the United States. He was certain he had done more for this country than any other United States President had ever done. If you talked to Mr. Gunter very long, Theodore Roosevelt's name was sure to come up. He would tolerate no negative statements about his hero.

To illustrate the depth of his admiration, he had named his daughter Theodora, to be called Theo. President Roosevelt had two sons named Archie and Quentin—then, so did Mr. Gunter. Archie Gunter died at a young age. But Quentin, who was always called "Clink" became a large and very handsome man. He worked to supplement the football scholarship he received to attend Murray State University, and he led a successful life.

At least Mr. Riley Gunter did not have a counterpart to Mr. Roosevelt's notorious daughter, Alice, who was best known as being tempestuous and ignoring the propriety expected of a daughter of a president. One day when she burst in on an important meeting in the White House, her exasperated father admitted, "I can either run this country or I can control Alice. I cannot do both!" Mr. Gunter did have an older daughter, Ruth. One can only speculate if her name was in any way connected to the Roosevelts.

Theo, in her early 20's, was an attractive girl, but might be best described as cute rather than pretty. Her friends would say she was sweet and sassy. With curly auburn hair and a heavy sprinkling of freckles, she had an endearing personality, outgoing and vivacious. Though very friendly and fun loving, her behavior was always socially acceptable.

Ruth, however was the antithesis of her sister, in that she was very somber, quite suspicious of other people's motives, and a bit on the pessimistic end of the spectrum. But she was beautiful with coal black hair, and the loveliest complexion. Everyone remarked on her skin, describing it as looking like a gardenia blossom, creamy white, with a tinge of pink on her prominent cheekbones. Both girls had gray eyes, tinged with blue, that seemed to change color, reflecting whatever color of clothing they wore.

The Gunter family lived in Paducah, but often visited their Aunt Amelia, affectionately known as Mealie, who lived in Wiswell.

Early in World War II, a troop train came through, stopping briefly in Paducah, though the soldiers didn't get off while there. As was their usual approach to fulfilling their Christian obligations, a Missionary Society made up of young ladies from a Paducah Methodist Church, were prepared to minister to the soldiers by providing them with a huge basket of baked goodies to pass around. Theo was a member of this group and participated by baking her famous Pecan Praline Fudge Bars. A double batch! Everyone had tried to out-do themselves, and spared no expense or effort. At that point, sugar had not yet been rationed.

The ladies went to the depot where the train was awaiting orders to continue its journey. The basket of individually wrapped treats was given to the Lieutenant to pass among the enlisted men onboard. He thanked them profusely, then added that he had a request. "My men are going to be a long way from home. They will be homesick and missing their family and friends. They would love to get letters from home, or from anyone, actually, even if it's just like a pen pal. When they heard that you ladies were coming, they came up with the idea of writing their names and addresses, in care of the army, on pieces of paper and throwing them out here on the ground. I hope that each of you will be so kind as to pick up one of the names and respond."

When the scraps of paper came flying out Theo reached down and picked up one of them. The name was Martin Schriener, and along the edge he had written "They call me Matt."

Ruth sniffed, to show her displeasure, and said, "Surely you're not going to write to him."

"Yes, I am. What can it hurt? You heard the officer say it would just be like a pen pal. I know I'll probably never see him. I might not ever even hear from him, but I will write him a letter."

Ruth looked at the name on the paper and exclaimed, "Schriener! Why that's a German name." Not recognizing that her own name, Gunter, was also German. "He may be a spy. Maybe he joined up so he can murder the other boys, just waiting till the best time to do the evil deed."

Theo did write Matt, and he did reply, and then they corresponded often. He told her that he lived on the east river in Flushing, New York. That he was a carpenter, like his father, and they were in the business of building boats. His parents had emigrated from Germany, but he had been born in the United States. He also told her that he wanted to come meet her in person, as well as her family. So, plans were made for him to come when he got his furlough immediately prior to being shipped to the war zones overseas. Things were beginning to get serious between the young couple, though as yet neither of them had actually seen the other.

And so, Matt came to visit and stayed in the guest room. Ruth was very perturbed. "He's a full-blooded German. What if he is coming here to murder us in our sleep."

Furthermore, she greatly resented the fact that, since sugar had just become rationed, that they had saved their sugar rations, and then splurged it all to make a pecan pie for him so he could taste true southern cooking.

It was about this time that there was a major fire in Paducah, and then a bank in Murray burned. Next there was a fire at nearby Murray High School. It was reported that there was a strong suspicion that the fires were part of an espionage act. There was much concern that a foreign spy was living amongst us. Ruth thought this gave credence to her fear.

It was during this visit that a friend took a snapshot of the ever-happy-go-lucky Theo wearing Matt's uniform, with his duffel bag slung over her shoulder. Ruth could be seen in the distant background with a scowl on her face.

After the war, Matt came to Paducah and he and Theo were married. She wore a street length white dress, white shoes, and a white hat. She carried a bouquet of white roses from Aunt Mealie's flower garden. After the wedding they moved to New York and lived with his parents. He returned to work with his father in carpentry. The after-war boom created a great deal of building work for him.

After some time, Theo wrote her Aunt Mealie saying that her husband so wanted to be a farmer. She asked if she and Matt could come stay with her so that Uncle Tom could teach him how to farm.

Ruth warned them that Wiswell residents would not be welcoming to him, a Yankee with a northern accent and German name. It was even possible that he might be Catholic. This area was sometimes described by non-residents as provincial and not warm and receptive to sojourners, or those who "are not from around here" as some would say.

But she was wrong. They came to Wiswell and lived with her Aunt Mealie and Uncle Tom. Matt was readily accepted. He fit in well with the local residents and learned to farm using mules, as Uncle Tom did not have a tractor or any modern farm equipment. He faithfully attended church services at South Pleasant Grove United Methodist Church, with the Erwin family. He became good friends and fishing buddies with several of the neighbors. Matt was living his dream as a farmer.

But guess what. While Matt and Uncle Tom were getting along splendidly, Theo and Aunt Mealie were having discord. One of those "two women in the same household" sort of thing. It was not known exactly what the friction was about, but it was known that Amelia was a very strong woman. She had been a spinster when she married Tom, but not because she had not been asked. She had spurned some earlier offers because marriage proposals were usually from widowers needing help raising their children. "I'll never raise anyone's children but my own," she said, emphatically.

So even though Matt loved farming he gave it up and they moved back to New York.

Theo was killed in a car crash in 1964, and was brought back to Wiswell and buried at South Pleasant Grove United Methodist Church.

A few years later, Matt married Emma, Theo's best friend from Illinois, and they lived in New York. When they came to visit her family in Illinois, they would continue on to Wiswell where they would visit with Theo's family. Emma also became friends with Theo's relatives, and remembered Theo's cousin, Imogene Paschall, by bequeathing her large collection of depression glass to her.

Matt died in 1990. He had requested that he be buried beside Theo at South Pleasant Grove United Methodist Church Cemetery in Wiswell. He had said, "I want to be planted beside Theo so I can be close to her family."

Some of his family from New York came for his funeral and were put up at Theo's relatives' homes, where they were served delicious home cooked meals. They voiced amazement at the southern hospitality that they were shown.

So that is how a little strip of paper containing a young soldier's name and address, thrown out the window of a troop train, meant to create a pen pal relationship, blossomed into a romance that became a life-long love story.

Sunday afternoon Sports

On Sunday afternoons, after church and after dinner, many of the neighborhood boys would congregate at our house to play and discuss sports. Harold Hopper, and his little brother, Bobby, as well as Joe Milton Brandon, and maybe Hazel Lee Boyd were nearly always present. My cousin, Harry, who came with his family for dinner every Sunday, was welcomed to play with them. Though he was only nine months older than me, I was not allowed to play, and was frequently reminded that I was too little. I knew Harry and I were the same size because when his mother, my Aunt Virginia, an accomplished seamstress, made a dress for me, and I was not there to try it on, she made Harry put it on to make sure she got the hem even. And it just fit him, like it fit me. But, despite my pleading Mama would not make them let me play, and heaven knows I begged her incessantly. Sometimes when they played baseball, they would let me chase down a foul ball. But I never got to bat.

My brothers Lynn and Hugh Thomas had the sports gear necessary for their games. For a basketball goal they used an old discarded milk bucket. Its rusted-out bottom had been filed away to smooth edges. Though the diameter of the goal was not exactly kosher, it was nailed to the south side of the smoke house at regulation height; the top of the hoop was precisely 10 feet from the ground, the same as specified by the NBA, an organization which had recently been formed and served as a standard for all basketball courts everywhere. To keep the dimensions in proportion, a tennis ball was substituted for a basketball, considering the small diameter of the goal.

In the summer time they were more likely to play baseball. The Wilkerson boys were proud owners of a real baseball, a legitimate Louisville Slugger bat, and a genuine leather mitt, paid for with their own money earned by working as hired hands in neighbors' fields.

When all the players had arrived, they were tempted to just listen to the St. Louis Cardinals baseball game that was just coming on the radio, instead of playing themselves. This was everybody's favorite team, and Enos Slaughter was their favorite player. They idolized him. He was their hero two times over. First, he led the Cardinals to the world Series victory in 1942. Second, he did his patriotic duty by serving in the Armed Forces for three years. Now he was back with the Red Birds, right where he had left off, and it looked like he was leading his team to another World Series Championship. Furthermore, he was apparently a farm lad, as his nickname was "Country" which endeared him even more to these farm boys who fancied themselves baseball players of some regard too.

To compromise, or perhaps I should say to make the best of both worlds, they decided they would do both: listen to the broadcast and play their own game. Lynn got a long extension cord and brought the radio outside and placed it on the front porch swing. He turned on the game, blaring at full amplitude. Then they played their game with the same enthusiasm, as they would have if Enos Slaughter was there in person

When the Cardinal game was over, and the sportscaster, Harry Caray had yelled "Holy Cow," for the last time that day, the Wiswell team had finished their game too.

"I'm hungry!" Joe Milton said

"Me, too," they all agreed, in unison.

"I know where there're some apples. Mr. Porter Bradley has an orchard of little sweet pears and several apple trees. We could all go get us a couple apples to eat. He'd never miss a few apples; he has about a dozen trees. And they're loaded."

"It's broad open daylight. He'll see us," warned one of the boys.

"Not if we go around the back way. Come on. Let's go."

They took off running and went the long way around, being careful to stay out of view. As they came up to the back fence, the orchard came into sight. There were trees with yellow apples, some with red apples, and one with green apples.

"Oh, those apples look so sweet!" Hugh Thomas said

"I like the sour apples best," Bobby voiced his preference. "I'm heading for the green apples. I wish I had brought some salt to sprinkle on mine. That would make them even more sour." And he puckered his mouth up, in anticipation.

Lynn said, "I wish we had brought a paper sack. The apples won't fit in my pocket."

After a while Harold said "I know what to do. Bobby is wearing bib overalls. Somebody, give me your shoestrings. I've got an idea!"

He gathered up the bottoms of the little overall legs and bound them tight with the shoe strings. Then they all joined in dropping apples into Bobby's pants from the top. Soon his overalls were bulging full from top to bottom. It was surprising how many it held.

Just then Mr. Bradley's dog began barking. It was obvious it was coming in their direction.

"We'd better run!" someone said, and they all started at top speed, with little Bobby struggling to keep up. As they approached the fence, Harold pulled up on the bottom row of barbed wire, and each boy bent over low, crouching, and managed to crawl under the fence—except Bobby. With all the apples in his pants, he was stiff as a board. He could not even bend to try to get under the fence. The dog was getting closer. Harold dropped the fence and ran off with the other boys.

Bobby fell to the ground and couldn't get himself upright. The dog was upon him, as Bobby squeezed his eyes tight, awaiting whatever the dog--or its owner—might do to him. The dog had quit barking. Bobby opened his eyes, and he could see the big dog, wagging its tail, and it began to lick the apple juice from his face.

Mr. Bradley had arrived beside the dog, and he pulled the boy to his feet. "Well, it's little Bobby Hopper, trying to steal some apples from me, eh? Or maybe you've just picked some apples for me, young man? Come to the house with me."

Bobby had to walk stiff-legged, but he trudged on. When they arrived at the house, the farmer removed the shoestrings and helped shake the apples out onto the ground. "I sure do thank you for picking some apples for me," he laughed. "Guess the Missus will bake a pie for supper. Now run along." Little Bobby could not run fast enough, but before he had gone very far, he was called back.

"Minnie," the farmer turned back facing the house, and called out. "Bring me a paper sack." When it arrived, he put several apples in it and handed it to Bobby.

"Any time you want some apples, just come to my front door. I'll be happy for you to pick some. Don't sneak under the back fence. And tell your buddies the same goes for them."

Bobby thanked him. But he never went back to the orchard.

A Gift for a Gift

Mrs. Jewel had been feeling poorly, and her neighbor, Shirley Russell, who was also a long-time close friend, called to hear from her. Always optimistic, Mrs. Jewel, when asked, said she was tolerably well.

Shirley suspected that her friend might benefit from a little special attention, so she gathered her three daughters together and solicited their help in doing something nice for Mrs. Jewel. "She has always been like a Grandmother to me," she told the girls.

"Let's make a cake for her," Kay suggested.

"Yes, a Bundt cake," said Krista.

They got the ingredients together and the girls helped bake the cake. They made the seven-minute frosting, which requires the use of a double boiler, and is difficult to get the exact consistency. This time the icing turned out perfectly, snow white and fluffy.

"I'll get the Tupper Ware cake carrier," offered Karla, as soon as the cake was cooled. And she got the little step stool and pushed it up tight to the cupboard. She could still only barely reach the container, but she completed the mission successfully. Carrying the cake gingerly to the car, Shirley drove to Mrs. Jewel's house, and surprised her with the cake.

It was an unspoken rule in the Wiswell Community, or at least in Mrs. Jewel's house, that a gift requires a gift in return. The cake was cut and enjoyed. After a while, when her guests were ready to leave, Mrs. Jewel seemed to be searching the room for something.

"What can I give Shirley?" she thought to herself. "They went to all that trouble and surprised me with a cake. I must come up with something. After all, I want to set an example of proper manners before these little girls. I will be ashamed to take the cake they went to so much trouble to bake for me, and then let them leave empty-handed."

She was getting desperate, but finally, she hit on an idea of how to reciprocate, and her face broke into a smile. She said, "I want to give you a cutting from my Christmas Cactus." Her plant was large and still in full bloom, in early January. Pink clusters of blossoms attached to green stalks draped down over the pot. She proceeded to break off a piece of the plant.

Shirley transplanted the Christmas Cactus, which grew into a beautiful plant filling a large pot, and blooming faithfully every Christmas. It sets in the South window of Shirley's living room, where it serves as a constant reminder of Mrs. Jewel. Though they say that no reminder is needed.

Twilight

That wonderful, peaceful time between sunset and dark was always my favorite time of the day. I called it twilight. The last gentle light of the day came through the window, suffusing everything with a golden glow. It gave me a feeling of comfort and I felt safe, and with family around me, I felt cared for.

I was home. The joy I felt took my breath away.

We would all congregate at the supper table, and we usually had a light supper, leftovers from dinner, which had been a big meal. Or we might just have corn bread and buttermilk, and maybe some baked sweet potatoes, still warm, from the oven. After supper we would gather in the living room. If a new quilt was in the frame, as was often the case, it would be raised to the ceiling, to make room for all seven of us.

Sometimes we played a modified version of a card game called Authors. The original game was a deck of cards consisting of nine sets of four cards, each set had pictures of one different author. The cards were shuffled and placed face down, and turns were taken drawing and then discarding a card. The object was to get complete sets of four alike; whoever matched the most sets won. While we never had the actual Authors card game, we, as usual, learned to use our own ingenuity and made our own cards. In election years, all the local candidates made multiple visits to everyone's doors to request their vote, and they gave a "candidate card" which was about the size of a regular playing card. It had his picture on it, along with his slogan, usually something like 'The best man for the job' and it almost always was a man. If no one was home, the card was left tucked in the door. If necessary, we would trade cards with other children who were also trying to build a set of cards. For example, if we had five "Seth Cooper For Jailer" cards, we might trade one for a "Charlie Marr For Sheriff" card to complete that set. So instead of pictures of authors, our cards had pictures of the candidates. Often the cards, though well-worn, lasted much longer than many of the candidates' political careers.

We loved to listen to stories on the radio, but this was cut to a minimum during the war years, to conserve the life of the battery. We wanted to save the battery to hear news of the war, and we knew it might be impossible to purchase a new one. One radio program we all liked and did try to hear was *Jack Armstrong, the All-American Boy*. It was sponsored by General Mills, and we heard the benefits obtained by eating their breakfast cereal from Jack, himself. "Wheaties, the breakfast of Champions," he said in a convincing tone of voice. We figured if the American boy ate the cereal it would be the patriotic thing for us to follow suit. We had begged Mama to get some for us, and we knew the peddler carried them on his truck. But she would only listen to our plea if we were feeling puny, and then we ate them straight from the box.

It was always fun to play I Spy, or similar games, altered to fit our life style. Other times we just talked about the happenings of the day. Lynn and Hugh had started playing basketball on the Junior Varsity team, and their conversation often centered on sports, either local or professional games that they heard on the radio.

If it was winter time, we would pull our chairs into a semi-circle around the fireplace. Someone would often volunteer to make some popcorn.

"Be sure and put some goobers in with the popcorn," Hugh Thomas always requested. We raised our own popcorn and peanuts, and we used our homemade butter, or if we wanted something really delicious, instead of butter we would use bacon drippings.

Our popcorn popper was a square metal box with a sliding lid on top. It was attached to a long wooden handle, so the user could hold the popper over the open fire, keeping a distance, and without burning his hands.

I always wanted to make the popcorn, but I wasn't allowed to get that close to the open fireplace. My request to do so was always met by someone saying, "You're too little." It seemed it was the story of my life.

Sometimes Rebecca and Iva would decide to make popcorn balls. They would cook down some molasses until it was even thicker, then pour this confection over some freshly popped popcorn. They would grease their hands with butter, pick up a hand full and squeeze it together and work it into a ball, then place them on a sheet of wax paper. They didn't stay there long. They were so good. They looked and tasted just like the Cracker Jacks that we saw at Wiswell Country Store, with the picture of the little boy in his sailor suit with his little doggie. The slogan, "The more you eat, the more you want" was printed on the box. The only difference was that our popcorn balls didn't have a toy in them.

Time went on. Season followed season. I had started to school, and I loved learning. When I was in the second grade, we had to share our room, and our teacher, with the first grade. Since my older sisters had already taught me to read before I even started to school, I was known to be a voracious reader. Consequently, the teacher enlisted my help in teaching the first-graders how to read. But my real goal in going to school was playing with my friends. I spent many over-night visits with girlfriends, and even more commonly, a girlfriend would come home with me on my school bus to spend the night.

But tonight, it was just our family together. It was a cold day, and we were all sitting around the fireplace after supper. Outside the wind was howling around the corner of the house, and it even came down the chimney so that the fire fluttered a little. Papa had brought in some fire wood and placed it on the hearth. He got up and laid a couple of the logs in the fire. The ice on the logs began to make a sizzling sound as it met the fire.

Tonight, when the fire burned down to just glowing embers, Papa would bank the fire, by scattering a coating of ashes over the coals. This would cause the coals to become dormant and assure there would be live coals in the morning, so that just adding a little kindling would make the fire leap to life.

The lamp was setting on a nearby table. It had been filled with coal oil, the globe shined to a sparkle and the wick trimmed, ready, when the light from the fire dimmed.

As the new logs caught fire and blazed up, the room was well illuminated. It radiated warmth that was reflected in our mood, creating such a cozy feeling. There was a lull in the conversation; it was enough to just sit there for a while, in the calm and quiet. The family was connected in unity and love that needed no open declaration.

When the fire began to die down, and the room grew dark, Mama broke our reverie, "Somebody needs to get up and light the lamp."

I jumped up. "I'll do it. Oh, let me."

I waited to hear the old familiar, "You can't do it. You're too little."

Silently, but with a smile, Papa handed me the box of matches.

ACKNOWLEDGMENTS

I would like to recognize The Scribblers Writing Group, composed of the regulars, Gerry Mellon, Deborah Hale, Kathy Culbert, Liz Rose, Joni Duane, Wilma Sanders, Ruth Daughaday, and myself. Their critique of my writing was always in the form of encouragement. Thank you for laughing at all the funny parts, and more importantly, for not laughing at my more serious efforts.

There were many helpful suggestions by my Thursday Lunch Bunch, my colleagues, all retired from the Department of Nursing, Murray State University, Geneva Cooper, Sharon Myatt, and Jeanette Furchess.

I am grateful to my husband, Ray, who grew up in upstate New York, in more affluent surroundings, but who graciously listened to every chapter of my book, again and again, after each draft, and appeared to be extremely interested in what life was like in Wiswell during my childhood. By doing so, he seems to have adopted some of the nostalgic feelings into his own repertoire.

Many of my friends and neighbors contributed their own memories of days gone by, and in some instances shared letters and military documents regarding their family members.

Thank you to everyone who has purchased *Coming Home to Wiswell*, the first book in this series. I was heartened by your flattering comments, and they inspired me to write *You Can't Un-ring the Bell*, for which you tell me, you are awaiting with bated breath.

I would like to express my appreciation to the staff at BookBaby, for personalized attention, making certain that every detail is as I intended.

My 95 year-old sister, who just recently survived a positive diagnosis of Covid-19, while living in a nursing facility collaborated with me on the phone, confirming dates and names; so I say thank you, Iva Nel.

And, lastly, I would like to thank Mama, not just for the peach tree tea, but for her example of how a Christian life should be lived.

Photograph of author (back of cover)

Caption: The author, Linda Fay Clark, lives with her husband, Ray, and their two Shih Tsu dogs, Muffin and Scout, on the same farm in Wiswell where she was born at home 85 years ago.